Scotland Poets
Edited by Samantha Wood

Young**Writers**

First published in Great Britain in 2008 by:
Young Writers
Remus House
Coltsfoot Drive
Peterborough
PE2 9JX
Telephone: 01733 890066
Website: www.youngwriters.co.uk

SB ISBN 978-1 84431 754 7

Foreword

Young Writers' Big Green Poetry Machine is a showcase for our nation's most brilliant young poets to share their thoughts, hopes and fears for the planet they call home.

Young Writers was established in 1991 to nurture creativity in our children and young adults, to give them an interest in poetry and an outlet to express themselves. Seeing their work in print will encourage them to keep writing as they grow, and become our poets of tomorrow.

Selecting the poems has been challenging and immensely rewarding. The effort and imagination invested by these young writers makes their poems a pleasure to enjoy reading time and time again.

Contents

Keiran Crockett (10)   32
Emma Forster (10)   33
Kyle Bellu (11)   33
William Jones (10)   33
Lewis Watt (11)   34
Hayley McMillan (10)   34
Marc Smith (11)   35
Callum Ross Leitch (11)   35
Cameron McHarg (11)   35
Jessica Megan Boyd (10)   36

Birkhill Primary School, Angus
Cameron McDonald (10)   36
Andrea Goodman (9)   36
Verity Marshall (9)   37
Lauren Han (10)   37
Nicola Reid (9)   38
Amy Parr (10)   38
Stephanie Robertson (9)   38
Kyle Morrison (10)   39
Julia Zhao (9)   39
Adil Kamran (9)   39
Chloë Shaw (9)   40

Carmondean Primary School, Livingston
Jade Cook (11)   40
Bethany Gibbon (11)   41
Michael Smith (11)   41
Shelby Harrop (11)   42
Sean MacLeod (11)   42
Danyelle Stevens (11)   43
Dylan Robertson (11)   43
Nicole Serzhantova (12)   44

Castlehill Primary School, Cupar
Brad Marcus Lambie (10)   44
Katie Phillips (10)   45
Fiona Simpson (9)   46
Shane Wilson (10)   47
Callum Edgcumbe (10)   47
Jamie Watters (10)   47

Sean Tasker (10)	48
Chloe Stewart (9)	48
Miriam Wood (9)	49
Oskar Fraser-Krauss (10)	49
Laura Nairn (9)	49
Gemma Robb (10)	50
Trisha Cairney (9)	50
Eilidh Wood (9)	50
Andrew Harley (9)	51
Thomas Paterson (10)	51
Lori Cuthbert (9)	51
Gemma Todd (10)	52
Adam Scott Cook (10)	52
James Petrie (10)	52
Charlotte Hamilton (9)	53
Fionnlagh McGlashan (10)	53
Caitlin Robb (10)	54

Cuiken Primary School, Penicuik

Ross Mitchell (11)	55
Hannah Lawson (11)	55
Robert Brook (10)	55
Caitlin Dobbie (10)	56
Susan Greens (10)	56
Iain Jack Lawson (11)	57
Beth Gorrie (10)	57
Gemma Mack (11)	58
Matthew Garden (11)	58
Caela Jennifer Walker (11)	58
Becky Graham (11)	59
Aimie Sinton (10)	59
Zoe Zurbriggen (10)	59

Gowriehill Primary School, Dundee

Ciara Mitchell (10)	60
Sam Barclay (9)	60
Stuart Rae (9)	61
Sarah Georges (10)	61
Kelsey Mitchell (10)	62
Graham Thomas McGee (10)	62
Nicole Millar (9)	63

Jordan Winter (10)   63
Sarah O'Brien (10)   64
Darren Forbes (10)   64
Megan Charlie Grier (9)   64
Lauren Scott (10)   65
Ewan Kelly (9)   65

Halkirk Primary School, Caithness

Euan Munro (9)   65
Kirsty Robertson (10)   66
Tom Walker (10)   66
Bryony MacDonald (10)   67
Charlie Innes (9)   67
Bryony-Skye Sanderson (10)   68
Matthew Cowan (11)   68
Jennifer Don (10)   69
Jessica Florence (9)   69
Euan Bremner (10)   70
Ian Mackay (10)   70
Katie Macleod (9)   71
Brandon Brinded (10)   71
Isla Louise Cartwright (10)   71
Christopher Gunn (10)   72
Andrew David McLaren (10)   72
Erin Shearsmith (9)   73
Jack McKee (9)   73
Terri Liz Munro (8)   73
Louise Fraser (9)   74
Declan Gunn (9)   74
Craig Kennedy Yuille (9)   74
Lewis Sutherland (9)   75
Jamie Mackay (10)   75
Shaun Gunn (9)   75
Scott Yuille (9)   76
Charlie Firth (9)   76
Skye Rogerson (9)   76
Emma Coghill (10)   77
James Barry Brotherston (11)   77
Megan Mackay (10)   78
Elly Jackson (10)   78
James Alexander Mackintosh (8)   79

Hill Primary School, Blairgowrie

Bryan Rennie (11)	79
Heather Smith (11)	79
Alison Rae (11)	80
Briana Freed Smith (12)	80
Caitlin Mackenzie (11)	81
James Clarkson (11)	81
Daniel Duncan (11)	82

Iona Primary School, Argyll

Ben Black (10)	82

Kinglassie Primary School, Kinglassie

Zoe Graham (8)	83
Chelsea Leigh Hutchison (8)	83
Craig Harlow (8)	84
Lauren Paterson (9)	84
Ceira Knox (9)	85
Euan Watters (8)	85
William Pirrie (8)	86
Simone Sallan (9)	86
Emma Fotheringham (8)	86
Liam James Gay (9)	87
Taylor Thomson (8)	87
Kali Wright (8)	87
Breagha Kipling (9)	88
Rachel Carr (9)	88

Langbank Primary School, Langbank

Argyll McCoist (9)	89
Max Ashmore (9)	89
Marisa Diane Keegan (9)	89
Ross Eaglesham (9)	90
Ross Tyre (9)	90

Longforgan Primary School, Longforgan

Katie Joss (7)	91
Gavin Anderson (7)	91
Dylan Reid (8)	91
Lewis Hunter (7)	92

Beth McNeish (8)	92
Ben Dunmore (8)	92
Adam Cartwright (8)	93
Natalie McKinnie (7)	93
Charlotte Jennings (8)	94
Cameron Johnston (7)	94
Abby Lang (8)	95
Jamie Dunmore (8)	95

New Aberdour School, Fraserburgh

Susie Garratt (8)	96
Heather Perkins (9)	96
Ryan Borwick (8)	96

Park Place Primary School, Dundee

Dana Leslie (10)	97
Eden Miller (9)	98

Ravenscraig Primary School, Inverclyde

Rebecca Greig (11)	98
Ellis Cunningham (10)	99
Kiera Purdie (10)	99
Laura Fulton (10)	100
Robyn McGhee (10)	101
Beth MacGugan (10)	101
Ashleigh McCready (10)	102
Sophie Hunter (10)	102
Rebecca Quinn (10)	103

St Gabriel's RC Primary School, Greenock

Morgan McLatchie (7)	103
Cara Turner (6)	104
Jennifer Gray (7)	104

St Monica's Primary School, Kirkwood

Amie Louise Martin (9)	104
Aiden Ward (11)	105
Amy McSwiggan (11)	105
Rhiannon McEnroe (11)	106
Joseph Brannigan (11)	106

Darren Conway (11)   107
Elysha McLaughlin (11)   107
Jodie Hetherston (11)   108
Kiera Cullen (11)   108
Aiden Mackinnon (9)   109
Taylor McAllister (11)   109
Beckie McEwan (12)   110
Emma Robertson (11)   110
Kelsey Cullen (11)   111
Chloe Boyle (11)   111
Sean Fraser (11)   112
Shannon Morgan (11)   112

Sandbank Primary School, Dunoon
Rachel Mosley (9)   113
Chloe Carney (9)   113

Sikeside Primary School, Coatbridge
Jack Dempster (11)   114
Aidan Killen (11)   114
Linsey Henry (11)   115

Strathblane Primary School, Glasgow
Alexander Macrae (8)   115
Alessandro Palmarini & Innis Sherwood-Thompson (8)   116
Lucy Taylor Van Nimwegen & Jennifer Cruickshanks (8)   116
Calum McCutcheon (8) & Andrew Byles (9)   117
Alice Ferguson & Grace Currie (9)   117
Conor Haggerty & Martin Riis (8)   118
Fraser Maccorquodale (8)   118
Ross McGregor & Eddie Wallace (8)   118
Charlie McCarron & Richard Jack (9)   119
Erin Orla Howell & Morgan Bernadette Stirton (8)   119
Jessica Collie (9)   119
Adam Wilson (8) & Caspar Schwahn (9)   120

Strone of Cally Primary School, Blairgowerie
Craig Rimmer (10)   120

The Glasgow Academy Atholl, Glasgow

Lewis McLean (8)	120
Colin MacFarlane (8)	121
Iain Fletcher (7)	121
Jamie Stewart (8)	121
Emma Hunter (7)	122
Mary Potts (8)	122
Alexander Stewart (8)	122
Mark Wilson (8)	123
Jack Henry (8)	123
Walter Connolly-Wilkes (7)	123
Larissa Lawrie Macaloney (8)	124
Hugo McGregor (8)	124
Alice Macintyre-Béon (8)	124
Georgia Dunn (9)	125
Alexandra Ava Barber (8)	125
Trevor Ace (7)	125
Jack James McCready (8)	126
Robyn Spalding (8)	126
Gordon Stackhouse (8)	127
Ruairidh Russell (8)	127
Sophie Pell (8)	128
Rajeshwar Dhami (8)	128
Katie Watson (8)	129
Judith Arbuckle (7)	129
Ruth Miller (9)	130
Morna Ruth Sinclair (8)	130
Luca Giovanazzi (8)	131
Zander Grant (7)	131

The Poems

Water

W aves crash like whales talking
A nemones make me feel ticklish and warm in the cold sea air
T urtles crawl along the beach like dancers
    dancing the Nutcracker
E els make me squirm
R ight as rain I run home.

Finn Manders (8)
Aberfoyle Primary School, Stirling

Litterbug

Litter always makes me angry,
So don't just sit there, go and be handy.
Put your litter in the bin not on the ground
Or all the manky stuff you drop will be floating all around.
Rubbish can be dangerous to animals around you,
So all I say is, don't be mean, just be green.

Emily Palau (10)
Aberfoyle Primary School, Stirling

Help!

Help the gorillas, please, please, please help the gorillas.
You're poaching them, you killers,
You're using their hands as ashtrays.
The poor gorillas, they don't have a say,
So save the gorillas instead of poaching them, you killers,
They don't have the power, we do.

Lauren McIntyre (10)
Aberlady Primary School, Aberlady

Save The World

The rainforest is going,
It is disappearing,
The animals dead,
The tribes with no home.

Stop cutting down the trees,
We will stop killing the animals,
Give the tribes their home back,
Give the rainforest back.

Recycle paper and save trees,
Don't put it in the bin,
Don't put it into a hole in the ground,
It's better to recycle.

Come and help to recycle,
It's not too hard,
To be honest it's easy,
A small effort makes a big difference.

Lauchlan Aird (9)
Aberlady Primary School, Aberlady

The War

The war makes me feel sad and angry.
I would hate to be in the war with bombshells crashing down on me.
I would be shooting people on the streets of Afghanistan
And I don't agree with this!
Snipers in a house, shooting innocent people.
I just wish there could be peace between us
And make the world a better place.

Cameron Alexander (9)
Aberlady Primary School, Aberlady

Why, How And What?

Why do we have to kill the giant pandas?
How do you know if they're endangered?
It's very, very sad!
What do you think we could do to save them?

Why do you kill them? For their meat and skin?
They can't speak up to defend themselves, but we can!
China is saving them but we need to start!
Please, please help!
    Why, why, why?
How do you think we could save them?
They live on mountain slopes high above.
Leave them in peace, don't disturb their habitat.
    How, how, how?
What do you think they are doing?
No harm to us!
Give them bamboo, help them live.
They aren't killing us, we're killing them.
    What, what, what?

Ailidh Hamilton (10)
Aberlady Primary School, Aberlady

Stop Hunting!

Why do animals have to be killed?
Rhinos, polar bears, tigers and elephants,
Why, why, why?
Is it the joy of killing for tusks and skin?
Do the hunters jump for joy or shout hip hip hooray
When the sound of the gun brings the animals to its last legs?
Why, why, why?

Amy Currie (9)
Aberlady Primary School, Aberlady

Pollution

Pollution, pollution.
Just what will happen in the future?
Our place will just come down.
We might be underwater.
Nowhere to go.
We will just have to go someday.

Pollution, pollution.
One day the world will tear apart.
I will put a stop one day only if I am there.
Me and my friends will be there together.
In the mist, in the graveyard.
I am under my gravestone saying, 'Save the planet.'
I would like to be in a world without pollution.
As tears come down my cheeks,
I love the world!

Thea Melville (9)
Aberlady Primary School, Aberlady

Litter/Danger

L ook at the ground
I t is very important! Keep it clean
T ake the chance, save the planet
T he planet needs to be saved!
E mpty your pockets, don't drop it, *pick it up,* put it in the bin
R ecycle it if you can.

D on't kill the animals
A nimals matter
N ever damage the rainforests
G o for it, save the planet
E njoy the animals and people in the rainforest
R ainforests matter!

Rosie Isaac (9)
Aberlady Primary School, Aberlady

'No,' Said The Rainforest, 'No,' Said Recycling

Rainforest said,
'Rainforest is more important
because more trees are
being cut down by the minute.'

Recycling said, 'No!
Recycling is more important
because people need to recycle
because pollution is coming!'

Rainforest said, 'No!
Rainforest is more important
because half of the animals of the world
are in the rainforest,
half of the world's animals will be extinct.'

Recycling said, 'No!
Recycling is more important
because if most people recycle more,
pollute less the world will be a safer place!'

Joe Sampey (9)
Aberlady Primary School, Aberlady

Why?

Why does the world have to be full of pollution?
We want to breathe clean air, not choke on our air.
Why? Why? Why?
Why can't our world be full of peace and harmony,
So our world can be a free world, not a war world?
Why? Why? Why?
Why does the world have to be made of disease and poverty?
Everyone has the right to have medicine and money.
Why? Why? Why?
Why can't our world be a happy place?
Why? Why? Why?

Charlotte Doig (9)
Aberlady Primary School, Aberlady

On The Go

The monkey swings, the sloth is slow
but every single animal's on the go, go, go.
All the trees are chopping down,
ten million by the hour,
and every single animal has not one piece of power.
The monkey swings, the sloth is slow
but every single animal's on the go, go, go.
Some animals will scarcely escape,
others are not so lucky,
as they run away they scale an immense landscape.
The monkey swings, the sloth is slow
but every single animal's on the go, go, go.
We control the future, the future we control
so stop the trees getting chopped down,
the mystery we'll unroll.
The monkey swings, the sloth is slow
but every single animal's on the go, go, go.

Jack O'Malley (9)
Aberlady Primary School, Aberlady

Racism Makes Me Feel So Sad

Racism makes me feel sad,
Why can't we stop it now?
It does not matter if you're black or white,
Just think how you want to be treated,
As others want to be treated as well.

No wonder people go inside
'Cause people don't like to hear it,
So please can we just stop it now
And then I won't be so angry!

Ben Stirling (9)
Aberlady Primary School, Aberlady

The Wonderful World

The wonderful world is suffering
And it may be all our fault,
But if we all work together,
Pollution can come to a halt.
Let's recycle,
Use our brains,
So that in a few years,
The Earth will be more than remains.

The wonderful world, the excellent Earth,
Will be even more beautiful, with a little hard work.

Animals are dying,
This is bad,
Hunters are hunting,
Extinction is sad.

The wonderful world, the excellent Earth,
Will be even more beautiful, with a little hard work.

Daisy Chambers (10)
Aberlady Primary School, Aberlady

Homeless

H elp the homeless.
O ut in the cold when we're all warm in our houses.
M oney should be shared.
E veryone should be treated the same.
L onely people on their own.
E ating nice food is not an option for them.
S o wet when we're wrapped up and dry inside.
S o we should do something about it.

Daniel Hay (9)
Aberlady Primary School, Aberlady

Where Is The Love?

War is wrong
War is bad
War makes me angry
War makes me sad
Where is the love?

War is bad
The Earth is sad
Our hearts are low
So let's go, go, go!
Where is the love?

The cops can't do anything
So let's stop, stop, stop!
People got me thinking
Where is the love?

Kieran Young (10)
Aberlady Primary School, Aberlady

Save The Tiger

'Save the tiger,' you hear me shout.
Do not kill, think about what you're doing.
If you kill, soon the tiger will be gone.
Think, think, think.
100,000 Bengal tigers
Gone down to 4,000 because of us.
Angry, angry, angry, that's how I feel.
If you want to help raise money
Or go to the zoo
'Cause zoos raise a protest to the government,
So don't stay still, help!

Jack Alexander Hughes (9)
Aberlady Primary School, Aberlady

Why Do It?

War is bad
Fighting is sad
It makes us angry
Very, very angry.

War is bad
Fighting is sad
Think of the people
Dying, dying, dying.

War is bad
Fighting is sad
I want it to stop
To stop right now.

War is bad
Fighting is sad
What will happen in the future?
WW3, WW4, WW5, WW6,
So stop!

Calum Ward (9)
Aberlady Primary School, Aberlady

Help The Dolphins

D olphins are lovely animals, please do not hurt them.
O ut of the sea into the rescue centre they go.
L aughing hunters watch as the dolphins suffer deep down.
P oor dolphins, they can't shout for help.
H elp, please help, that is all we ask.
I think we should take action or
N ets catch and tangle in poor dolphins.
S ave, save, save the dolphins.

Laura Seaton (10)
Aberlady Primary School, Aberlady

The Polar Bears

T hud, thud, thud!
H ungrily she walks
E xtinction is close.

P ollution everywhere
O ver the ice
L ovingly she nudges her cubs
A nd lets them eat the last particles of food
R oaring with sadness for her land is disappearing.

B earing the hunger that haunts her stomach
E ver more water like a huge blue blanket
A stonished at her own skill she catches
   and eats part of the fish but shares with her cubs
R ough and tumble the cubs do play
S uch a special animal, yet what have we done to it?

Eleanor Dickson-Murray (9)
Aberlady Primary School, Aberlady

We Love The Planet

We love Planet Earth
Planet Earth loves us
But Planet Earth may hate us
For what we have done
The pollution in his seas
The heat that climate change can cause
We love Planet Earth but soon he may hate us
I want to save the planet
But that's only me!

Cairn Schulte (9)
Aberlady Primary School, Aberlady

Homeless

I was walking in town with my dad,
When I saw you,
You were quite old and dirty with a beard.
We walked on, I looked back,
I couldn't help it, my mouth dropped open.
Dad walked on.
Smelly old garbage cans, how do you live beside them?
The homeless beggar, begging for money.
I'd hate that. How did he get there?
I don't know.
I want someone to come and give them a house.
I can't. I hope they live good lives.

Callum Amos (8)
Achfary Primary School, Sutherland

I Cannot Bear It Anymore

I cannot bear it anymore.
The trees being cut down.
The animals extinct.
The rainforest destroyed!
I feel so mad!
It makes me wish I was a giant.
I'd stomp on all the people who are making this world a bad place.
Seeing tigers being hunted and many other creatures.
Hearing the chainsaw hacking fields of trees.
Sharing the sadness with the homeless animals.
We've gone too far.

Claire Barnes Miller (10)
Achfary Primary School, Sutherland

The Caring Tree

The tree has leaves that are falling,
The tree has branches that are breaking,
The tree has people around it,
The tree has some food to eat
And the tree has something to care for and that is the world.

It cares for the insects that live in its roots,
It cares for the bees that buzz on its leaves,
It cares for the butterflies that feed on its leaves,
It cares for the birds that nest on its branches,
It cares for the woodpecker that pecks on its trunk
And it cares for the children who play around it.

Ryan Jason Mollison (9)
Alyth Primary School, Alyth

Destruction

D on't drop litter
E veryone knows
S top and pick it up!
T read on it no more
R ecycle and reuse
U pset the world no more
C ola cans, pick them up
T he world is fading fast, please stop the pollution
I nsects crushed by diggers
O riginal features destroyed
N ations crushed in great numbers.

Daniel Burns (9)
Alyth Primary School, Alyth

The End Of The World

The end of the world
For the sweet little pandas
We should save them instead of having a war
We should lend a paw.

The end of the world
For the stripy big tigers
We should help them instead of snoring
We should be caring.

The start of death
For the tiny poor dodo
We should have saved them
Instead of not caring.

James Atkinson (9)
Alyth Primary School, Alyth

Pollution

P is for pollution which happens
O is for oceans far and wide
L is for leaves which we try to keep alive
L is for litter lying all round the street
U is for undoing the pollution
T is for tidy world we'd like
I is for I enjoy this tidy world
O is for our country to respect animals
N is for nature all around the world.

Linsey Macdonald (10)
Alyth Primary School, Alyth

Extinct

It is about time we stop this crime
The polar bears are dying
The iceberg turns to water that floats around the Arctic Ocean
The polar bear has nowhere to live, unlike us.

It is about time we stop this crime
The Siberian tiger is dying
The forest is getting cut down where they live
The Siberian tiger has no proper home, unlike us
We again cause this tragedy
All this is because of us!

Do we wait till all are extinct?
The bears and tigers who only want to live.

Ryan Duncan (9)
Alyth Primary School, Alyth

The World

T is for temperature the world is getting hot.
H is helping people trying to improve the world.
E is for electricity trying to run the world.

W is for water which poor countries need.
O is for oil which kills animals in the sea.
R is for rubbish getting worse every day.
L is for less food. Will it go round?
D is for dreadful which the world is going to be.

Amy Sangster (10)
Alyth Primary School, Alyth

The Dying Tree

I get used and wasted
My paper
In the bin
Chop here! Chop there!
I get replaced
With creatures inside me.
Houses on my roots
People kill me.

My family in the rainforest
Dying, maybe dead!
Their companions
The animals!
Losing us
Their homes
We all need each other
We are as one.

Recycling
Saves us
Instead people
Burn us
I am a tree
Now I am dead!

Euan Robb (10)
Alyth Primary School, Alyth

Litter

L is for the litter that is up on the hills and the beach.
I is for the people who ignore the signs and drop litter.
T is for the trees that are falling down.
T is for the tiny mini beasts that get stuck in cans
   and rubbish we drop.
E is for Europe that is very messy.
R is for rubbish that is taking over the world.

Kennedy Lee Muir (9)
Alyth Primary School, Alyth

Eco Rhyme

Plants
Trees
Bees
Live a happy life
Humans
Animals
Birds
Are part of our life
Tigers
Kangaroos
Bears
Live in fear of extinction.
The world is here to enjoy
Not to destroy!

Alexander Tosh (9)
Alyth Primary School, Alyth

Tree Life

T is for the twigs that help the birds build their nests
R is the rain that helps the tree grow
E is for the animal that eats the nuts off the tree
E for the egg that will hatch soon

L is for the tree to live forever and ever
I is for insects that live on trees
F is for the forest around about the tree
E is for the tree that gives energy to us all.

Kerri Younger (9)
Alyth Primary School, Alyth

Dolphins In Danger

Dolphins in danger, danger, danger.
Should not be caught in a net.
Get rid of that net, that net.
Save the dolphins, save them.
Dolphins smile, dolphins smile,
Get rid of that mucky pile.
Save our dolphins, keep them safe.
Dolphins here, dolphins there,
Dolphins everywhere.

Morgan Taylor (9)
Alyth Primary School, Alyth

Animals

A is for antelopes that look like deer,
   but become extinct every month and year.
N is for newts who live and die,
   who look like lizards but live near water.
I is for insects, ants, flies, butterflies and beetles
   but they are so small they get squashed!
M is for mammals - the warm-blooded animals.
A is for apes who get captured every day.
L is for leopards, large wild cats,
   who get shot every day and never come back.
S is for safari park where lions, elephants
   and other animals are safe from the hunting and killing.

Karen Arnold (10)
Alyth Primary School, Alyth

Extermination

The tigers are dying
The pandas are dying
Their habitats are falling
Oil is leaking into deep, deep oceans
Fish are dying
Birds aren't flying
Hunters are killing for food
Frogs and toads are getting squished on the road
Ice caps are melting, threatening the polar bears
Squirrels are dying because they are hungry
Because acorn trees are falling
This is madness for all these animals
Elephants are dying for their ivory tusks
Foxes are being used for rugs
Orang-utans' heads and hands
Are being hung up on some walls.

This is extermination!

Sam Flood (8)
Alyth Primary School, Alyth

Litter, Litter

Litter, litter why are you here?
The animals are gone, everything disappeared.
Litter, litter how did you get here?
My house is flooded, I have nothing to wear.
Litter, litter, I have such bad luck.
If you go I'll be as happy as a duck.
Litter, litter please disappear.
I'll beg for mercy then it will snow.
Thank you, thank you.
I hope you will agree it will be a better world if you go.
I'll have a good luck charm
I'll be happy if the world will change.

Rachell Campbell (9)
Alyth Primary School, Alyth

Just Rubbish

Rubbish here
Rubbish there
Rubbish is everywhere!

Rubbish on the hills
Rubbish on the beach
There should not be rubbish on our planet
Not even on the beach or anywhere!
Rubbish belongs in the bin.

Jack Dickson (9)
Alyth Primary School, Alyth

The War

Down in the bunker
Ready for war.
Bang, bang, boom!
People dying and people crying
But all you could hear was *bang, bang, boom!*
Everybody's sad,
Wives were sobbing their hearts out for them
But everybody knows why they went -
To save our country.
They said . . .

Matthew Mollison (9)
Alyth Primary School, Alyth

The Panda's Life

Pandas here, pandas there, pandas everywhere.
Pandas are born for life - black and white.
Come in all shapes and sizes, just like us.
Pandas like to eat bamboo, bamboo, very, very healthy too,
Pandas here, pandas there, pandas everywhere.

Brooke Kermack (9)
Alyth Primary School, Alyth

Litter About

L itter is all around us.
I t ruins people's lives.
T errible that's what it is.
T he wrappers take over the world.
E urope is getting very messy.
R educe, reuse, recycle today.

A ll the litter is piling up.
B ut some of us are tidying it up.
O n the streets, beach and everywhere.
U ntidy land, cement and sand.
T ell your friends to tidy up or you will have bad luck.

Meghan Bissett (9)
Alyth Primary School, Alyth

Don't Kill Mammals!

Why must hunters come along and destroy animals?
They're just as important as we are.
Just because the tiger has a fancy coat.
Why do hunters have to keep on killing them?
Why do hunters have to steal the pandas' bamboo?
The hunters just think they're smart.
P is for protection against the hunters.
We don't want hunters in our world do we.
Why must hunters hunt for orang-utans' paws and cut them off?
It's not fair on the lion because it's the king of the jungle!
The snow is melting quickly so try to keep it down.
The elephants are dying so don't steal the ivory.
The hunters don't understand about fish,
They're just another living thing.

Sean McInally (8)
Alyth Primary School, Alyth

I'm Dying

I am becoming extinct
So save me please,
Don't cut down any trees.
I am a panda and there is no bamboo
And it is all because of you.
Why do you kill us and use our fur,
For handbags, coats and many more?
The bamboo tree is my home
So please leave me alone.

Ailsa Bruce (8)
Alyth Primary School, Alyth

Put Your Litter In The Bin

People are polluting the world.
If people stopped dropping litter it would be a better place.
Litter is horrible. Don't drop your litter.
If you keep dropping litter you are polluting the world.
People have a recycling bin but they don't use it.
You are meant to take your rubbish out every day.
If you recycle it means less trees to cut down.

Ryan Bell (8)
Alyth Primary School, Alyth

My Life As An Orang-Utan

We are all dying
Because people are cutting down our homes
In the rainforest
To use for chairs and tables.
We are all becoming extinct
Because people are cutting off our hands and feet
To use as trophies on their walls.
Please help us.

Sarah Campbell (9)
Alyth Primary School, Alyth

I Am A Polar Bear

I am a polar bear
we are dying out.
This is really bad for us
since homes are warming up.
The ice cap is melting,
we will have to change
by getting used to warmer habitats.
This is very hard
in all sorts of different ways.
My cubs are getting hungry,
I feel like them,
my food is running out,
so please go on and help us
by recycling
lots and lots of things.

Hannah Oosterhoorn (9)
Alyth Primary School, Alyth

Mammals All Around The World

I am a tiger
My land is getting destroyed
Hunters are trying to find me
I am trying not to die
So I will run through the forest
So I will not be seen
So I am going to keep running
Through the forest.
Then I saw a hunter
Then I ran through the forest
As fast as I could then I got away.

Cameron Fraser (8)
Alyth Primary School, Alyth

Pollution

P is for people who are dropping litter.
O is for overheating, which if we don't recycle
the world will overheat.
L is for litter that people are dropping everywhere.
L is for landscape where hopefully there is no litter.
U is for unleaded petrol which reduces the pollution from vehicles.
T is for terrace where you normally find litter.
I is for infants who usually drop litter.
O is for oceans that are getting polluted.
N is for *no! Don't drop litter!*

Finlay Cook (9)
Alyth Primary School, Alyth

Litter

People dropping litter,
Doesn't make us any fitter,
Instead put it in the bin,
Then we will have a big grin.

Tom Haining (10)
Ardgour Primary School, Fort William

A Green World

Bits of paper and tins,
Make everywhere dirty,
We must pick them up,
To make the world nice and shiny.

Rebekah Connolly (5)
Ardgour Primary School, Fort William

Earth

Our Earth, this green orb,
This wonder of wonders,
Is under threat.
Our gases are bleeding,
The Earth to death.
Our cars and factories,
Are poisoning the skies.
Our plastic bags,
Are destroying the seas.
Greenhouse gases are infecting
The air we breathe.
The planet is changing
But there are things
We can do to help.
Start recycling,
Start today!

David Philip (9)
Ardgour Primary School, Fort William

Pollution

I'm in the sea, I'm in the air,
I'm on the land, I'm everywhere,
I have the power to turn buildings to dust,
I'm someone who you can't trust,
I've killed thousands of animals over the years,
Now in your eyes I see tears,
I pollute the air way up high,
I'm turning it into poison sky,
I disgust you don't I, well I'm called pollution,
But to defeat me there is a simple solution,
Turn things off and recycle.

Andrew Jackson (10)
Ardgour Primary School, Fort William

Poverty

There are poor people
Who are needing help from us
Dying all around
They want money for food
We all need to do something.

They are all alone
Begging people to help them
They are getting scraps
All we have to do is give
Give them all somewhere to live.

Jordan Hay (11)
Bervie Primary School, Inverbervie

Recycling

Keep Scotland tidy,
Do not be a litterbug,
Let us be a team,
Let's be a litter-free zone,
Be the good people we are.

People are awful,
How can we live with ourselves?
Yes, enjoy life now,
Do people know what's happening?
We can make a difference, think!
Do you have a heart?
People, the world is dying,
Let us take a stand,
Look around, everything gone,
Do something about it, help.

Shannon Crockett (11)
Bervie Primary School, Inverbervie

War Zone

Hell is here always,
Bang! Another person dead,
A depressing sight,
Dead soldiers, lying bloody,
People screaming and running.

Bang! A sudden scream,
Wounded, screaming for some help,
Bombs are going off,
Immense tankers everywhere,
Can we stop all of these deaths?

Rebecca Kalume (11)
Bervie Primary School, Inverbervie

War

You are in the war,
Guns and weapons all around.
I feel so alone.
Every corner that I take
I will be in great danger.

Look all around you,
In the bunkers and trenches,
There is no escape.
Think of all those poor people.
I can't explain how I feel.

Craig McKenzie (12)
Bervie Primary School, Inverbervie

War

Peace has been broken,
Bullets flying overhead,
Killing needlessly,
Men are dying in the street.
Will pain and grief ever end?

They storm the city,
Raining rubble and lost lives,
Slaughtering on sight,
Bombs raining down from the sky.
Will the fighting ever end?

Niall Alexander Boyd (11)
Bervie Primary School, Inverbervie

War

When will this war stop?
People dying everywhere,
Bombing is common,
Machine guns are everywhere.
This is a disgraceful war.

War is in Iraq,
Through cities, towns and mountains.
What shall they do now?
Planes flying, men swarming in,
Bombshells lying everywhere.

Our soldiers are brave,
Our men risking life and death.
Bring peace to the world!

Ashley Darling (11)
Bervie Primary School, Inverbervie

Litter

Litter comes in all shapes and sizes,
Malteser packets and even Mars bar boxes.
Even though we drop litter every day,
We can still put it away,
Or we might become litterbugs.
Now that *you* have heard the rhyme,
Maybe you won't do the crime.

Lewis Forbes (11)
Bervie Primary School, Inverbervie

Litter

Litter is yucky,
the sky is mucky.
What would we do if it was not yucky?
Would we treat it badly
or would we treat it well,
or would we just chuck the junk food?
We should help the Earth
and help it now
because tomorrow there might be a flood.

Stuart Smith (11)
Bervie Primary School, Inverbervie

Litter!

L ook around, what can you see?
I t's all litter, litter everywhere!
T oo many people making this mess
T oo late, the world is in distress!
E xcept for the people who have tried their best
R un around, picking up the litter
This is a warning you must take!

Abbie Shand (10)
Bervie Primary School, Inverbervie

The Rubbish Girl

We were playing with our friends,
wishing the day would never end,
when the girl came along,
doing things that were wrong.
Norma Pips was eating chips,
just as she always did.
She opened the bin and put them in,
not bothering to close the lid.
The litter got out and started to shout,
'Yay! We're free! Let's go!'
'You'd better put it back,' I said,
'look at that bit of mouldy bread!'
'I don't care if there's litter everywhere,
even if the animals get caught in the snare.'
I said, 'You better put it back in the bin,
before the teacher finds that tin.'
So she picked it up and put it back,
now Norma Pips, no more does she slack.

Eve Shepherd (11)
Bervie Primary School, Inverbervie

Our World

I breathe the pollution in the air,
The whales are in despair,
Help us now before the world becomes bare.
If you stop littering, which is one simple thing,
Maybe we can save everything.
And if it's not far
Don't use a car!
If we work together
We can save the world and remember,
Doing something little can make a big difference.

Alex Winters (10)
Bervie Primary School, Inverbervie

Save Our Planet

Save our planet, save our country,
Save our place from being mucky.
Don't drop litter, your litter,
Put it in the bin.
If you see litter
Pick it up and put it in the bin.
Please save our planet,
Please save our Earth,
Please save Scotland,
So it's eco-friendly.
Save our animals from becoming extinct,
Don't kill our country.
Pick up litter,
It only takes a second.
You will be a hero to our lovely world.

Daniel Eddie (11)
Bervie Primary School, Inverbervie

Litter

There's litter everywhere,
I wonder who would drop litter?
Maybe they think they're cool,
But there's nothing cool about dropping litter.
Why can't they just put it in the bin like everyone else?
Our school is being covered in litter
Because of these litterbugs.
We should do something about this!

Callum Morrison (11)
Bervie Primary School, Inverbervie

Scotland, Have Pride

Scotland, have pride
Oh please have pride,
Look at our streets,
Muck and grime.
When it comes to litter
We should really pick it up.
It only takes a sec
To save a part of our world.
You may be big, you may be small
But it doesn't really matter at all.
Just be a hero to all
By putting the litter in the bin.
We get acid rain, we go and complain
But it's our own fault.
Our animals are hurt from the glass we drop
So have some pride and pick it up.

Shaun Walker (11)
Bervie Primary School, Inverbervie

Litter

Litter here, litter there, litter is everywhere,
On the table and on the chair, should it be there?
My brother saw a Coke can and stuck his finger in there
So my daddy had to pull it out and put on a plaster.
Litter on the street, litter on the road,
Why do so many people drop their litter?
It makes a world a misery.
Don't be a fool, dropping litter is not cool.

Sophie Smith (10)
Bervie Primary School, Inverbervie

What Are You Doing?

What are you doing?
Mother Nature's dying!
There are fewer plants
And some birds aren't flying!

It's getting hotter
And I don't find it fair.
It is because
We're polluting the air.

Rainforests cut down
And plants that die.
Gives me a frown
And makes me sigh.

Stop pollution
And a shortage of rice.
Otherwise,
You'll pay a price!

Barnaby Simpkin (11)
Bervie Primary School, Inverbervie

Global Warming

The air is warning that global warming
Is spreading through the air.
It's getting hotter,
The world is getting slaughtered.
Now you know that we need help
And if you read the rhyme,
Please don't do the crime.

Keiran Crockett (10)
Bervie Primary School, Inverbervie

Save Our World, Save Our People

Recycling is cool, recycling rules!
Littering drools, littering, 'Boo!'
Polluting is the worst, it will kill us all!
Now you know, why do you do it?
It's a pity, so why don't you *stop it!*
Think of the world, grey and small,
It won't be good at all!
No more oxygen,
Polluted air.
It is so bad that animals and people can't bear it!

Emma Forster (10)
Bervie Primary School, Inverbervie

Our Changing World

Our world is changing very fast
and if we don't move now it'll be our last.
All of nature is withering away.
The human race has done all this, they must pay.
Up in the north, the ice is melting
but down in the south the rain is pelting.
All of this is caused by global warming
which means it'll be hotter in the morning.

Kyle Bellu (11)
Bervie Primary School, Inverbervie

Why?

Why be bitter and drop your litter?
Why leave on the light when it is very bright?
Why think it's cool to try and pollute?
Why cut down some trees when they are so very green?
Why use the car when it is not far?
Why?

William Jones (10)
Bervie Primary School, Inverbervie

Eco-Friendly Poem

B is for bright, when you don't need the light
E is for eco - so be it today

E is for eating wrappers, don't drop them on the ground
C is for can - so you can be eco-friendly
O is for ocean, so don't dump stuff in it

F is for friends, protect them as well
R is for recycling - this is very good
I is for information on eco, so read it
E is for ever - so don't ever forget to be eco
N is for no - say, 'No, litter should not be on the ground'
D is for dumping - so please don't do it
L is for leave - so leave plants where they are
Y is for you - so can you please be eco-friendly?

Lewis Watt (11)
Bervie Primary School, Inverbervie

Recycling

I see the lovely green, green grass
But in that mass of grass
I see a horrible sight,
With all my might,
The thing I see is litter.
Oh how bitter
Can people be to our country.
Plastic can be reused,
So let's get it moved.
Don't lie in bed,
Soon the world will be dead.
Everything will be gone,
Not that long.

Hayley McMillan (10)
Bervie Primary School, Inverbervie

Litter

I can smell the litter on the ground.
I can taste the apple core in the bin.
I can see lots and lots of litter on the ground
And I hope it goes in the bin.
I touch the litter and I put it in the bin.
I hear people eating their crisps.

Marc Smith (11)
Bervie Primary School, Inverbervie

A Green, Green Leaf

As we get happier
The planet gets hotter.
Ice caps fall
And no more snow for us.
There is no escape from it.
One thing can make a difference to our planet.
Just save fuel and keep happy,
Save nappies.
One thing makes so much difference.

Callum Ross Leitch (11)
Bervie Primary School, Inverbervie

Litter

Why do we drop litter?
It is not cool.
It harms the Earth.
It kills foxes, rabbits, birds and stoats,
So if you drop litter you are a fool.
Litter is disgusting.
Litter should be binned.
Let's give the litter-pickers a break.

Cameron McHarg (11)
Bervie Primary School, Inverbervie

We've Got To Fix It

As I step outside and open my eyes
I see the grass as the Earth's great mask.
I turn around and hear the sound of birds singing
and I see litter on the ground.
I taste and smell Mother Nature's world.
As I touch the world passing by,
it's us who's doing this,
so now it's our chance to do something and fix it.

Jessica Megan Boyd (10)
Bervie Primary School, Inverbervie

Cameron's Plea

Reuse your own bags
And save your old rags.
I just want to save the environment,
Now it will be time well spent.
Feel good because now I am reusing
Or I'm feeling bad because I am refusing.
Reduce all the cars out and about.
Soon enough we can change the world's fate.
Trees can be saved if you do all this.

Cameron McDonald (10)
Birkhill Primary School, Angus

Our World

Look at our world, it's dirty and mad
Our treasured polar bears are very sad
Ice is melting, it's going to be hot
If you don't *fight* to help our world
It will all be gone in a wind hurl
We can save it, help it, make it a better place
If you can't recycle it, reuse it
Put a smile upon his face.

Andrea Goodman (9)
Birkhill Primary School, Angus

Reduce, Reuse, Recycle

The world's in danger, can't you see?
Come and help save the world with me!
Everyone can do it, it's easy as can be,
Let's start with the R's, one, two and three.
The first R is reduce, let's see what we can do,
You just need to use less packaging,
It's all up to you!
The second R is reuse, just use things more than twice,
A bottle as a vase would be very nice.
The third is recycle, don't put stuff in the bin,
That will help to save the world
Then everyone will *grin!*

Verity Marshall (9)
Birkhill Primary School, Angus

Reuse, Reduce, Recycle

It's not too late
to decide the world's fate,
so come on people, let's concentrate.

Recycle cans and bottles too,
here's some examples; conditioner and shampoo.
Just doing that can save the world,
there's a couple of steps but let's get it fulfilled.

Reuse rubber, paper and plastic
and it will be like magic.
Just do your bit,
to keep you fit and nothing bad will happen.

Reduce the number of cars on roads
and then we can help animals like tadpoles and toads.
Never can we not jog or walk
but we can speak our minds and talk our thoughts.

Lauren Han (10)
Birkhill Primary School, Angus

Our Planet

Reduce the amount of electricity we use!
Everyone, do your bit for the environment!
Do your bit to save the planet!
Use plastic bottles and containers again!
Save our planet by recycling, reducing and reusing!
Every person can recycle!

Nicola Reid (9)
Birkhill Primary School, Angus

Reduce

R educe the use of plastic bags
E veryone can help
D oing your part is important
U se less plastic
C ut back on tins and bottles of juice
E veryone can sit down when the world is clean.

Amy Parr (10)
Birkhill Primary School, Angus

Recycle, Reduce, Reuse

R eady to recycle?
E veryone reduce!
C ome on get your slippers on and go and reuse!
Y ou make the world a tip now you have to clear it up!
C hoose the way the world should be!
L et's get working and clean with glee!
E very day you go shopping, buy things with less packaging!

Stephanie Robertson (9)
Birkhill Primary School, Angus

Recycle

Save the world by recycling,
Better weather for farming,
No pollution in the air,
So don't relax on a rocking chair,
So start running and . . .
Recycling!

Kyle Morrison (10)
Birkhill Primary School, Angus

Recycle

Get your act together
Recycling can change your life forever
Remember to not litter
If you do you are a twitter
Go green
Don't be mean to the great machine!

Julia Zhao (9)
Birkhill Primary School, Angus

Recycle

R educe, reuse, recycle!
E veryone can do it!
C artons, cans and paper!
Y ou can join in saving the environment!
C ome on everyone, we can try it!
L et's stop pollution!
E ncourage people to *recycle!*

Adil Kamran (9)
Birkhill Primary School, Angus

Save The Planet

Can you help to save the place?
Because this is such a disgrace.
Poverty, litter, rainforest and war.
Can you help to save them all?
Do your bit and you will be fit.
Come and save the place.

Chloë Shaw (9)
Birkhill Primary School, Angus

Polluted Rivers

P eople are dumping things in the rivers
O n the bottom of the river lies all the things that we have thrown.
L ots of us want to help.
L ots of people in the world, they don't really care.
U sually when we walk we dump things in there.
T alk to the people who are doing this, tell them to stop.
E veryone should stop polluting these rivers,
  they have done no harm.
D oing all these things is also hurting the animals like the little fish.

R ivers all over the world are getting polluted really bad.
I f we stop we can save the fish and we will have good clean
  rivers again.
V ery little is being done, there is not much to do.
E nd this pollution, make it stop.
R ealise what you have done to these rivers,
  they don't look very clean.
S end this message around, it needs to stop!

Jade Cook (11)
Carmondean Primary School, Livingston

A World Dustbin

A ll this world is mostly good at being a big dustbin,

W hatever this world seems to do it never seems to work,
O h all those wasted dustbins, dumpers and trash cans,
R eally, I mean come on,
L ook at what we have done,
D on't leave it, take action now.

D ustbins can't help that much,
U nderneath this world it is probably cleaner,
S till they might not use the same stuff as us,
T ogether we can take action now,
B ut we can only do it together,
I nstead of using the world as a dustbin,
N ote in your diary 'use proper bins'.

Bethany Gibbon (11)
Carmondean Primary School, Livingston

River Pollution

R ivers are being polluted
I t's killing lots of fish
V ery large amounts
E very object chucked in the river does have an effect
R ivers are being polluted

P ollution, not so good
O ften because of river pollution
L ots of fish are dying
L ittle ducks and swans as well
U nless you are a victim
T hanks to people not caring for rivers
I t's causing them to pollute the air
O ften making people ill that stay near a river
N ow we should all help and stop river pollution!

Michael Smith (11)
Carmondean Primary School, Livingston

Polluted Rivers

P eople are dumping their rubbish into rivers.
O il can pollute the rivers.
L ife for animals shouldn't be this way.
L ife is terrible I always say.
U nder water are fish and they could get hurt.
T ins and other pieces of junk are dangerous.
E very piece of can has a sharp edge.
D id you know it makes the place untidy?

R ivers can have fish in them.
I t is a curious matter.
V ery little people notice this problem.
E veryone's trying but we need more help.
R ivers and lakes are all affected by lots of junk.
S ome animals get hurt by the rubbish.

Shelby Harrop (11)
Carmondean Primary School, Livingston

Pollution

P ollution is spreading all over the world.
O ver the seas, killing trees.
L ying in the seas.
L ife is made to enjoy not to smell dumped litter and oil.
U nder the Earth, in our grass, killing our wildlife.
T o some people this is a problem for others another day.
I f we work as a team we can live a longer life.
O n the land-killing Earth
N ow is the time to stop littering and polluting.

Sean MacLeod (11)
Carmondean Primary School, Livingston

Pollution

P eople using hairspray and all the other gases polluting the air.
O ver the world people are not putting their rubbish in the bin,
soon we won't see the ground.
L akes, rivers, waters, seas and streams, they aren't crystal clean.
They are the most horrible colour I have ever seen.
L ovely little raindrops, so beautiful to watch but I have to be
careful, they will burn right through my skin.
U sually people don't worry but I can't help it, I like things
the way they're meant to be.
T rees are dying because we're wasting paper.
I n the world we could make a difference and get rid of pollution.
O h how hot, today is 30°C in December. I wish they'd fix that
hole in the ozone layer.
N owhere I can go to escape pollution.

Danyelle Stevens (11)
Carmondean Primary School, Livingston

Acid Rain

A cid rain, acid rain, go away, come again another day.
C hemicals are in the air, blowing everywhere to burn your skin.
I n the air it affects everywhere.
D anger is in the air, don't breathe it in.

R ain pollutes the air when people stop and stare.
A cid rain mostly affects Russia.
I hate acid rain, nobody likes it.
N ever come back again acid rain.

Dylan Robertson (11)
Carmondean Primary School, Livingston

Acid Rain

A ll the time I see the rain it makes me feel quite sad.
C ome a rainstorm and it is very, very bad.
I like the sunlight touching my skin.
D ust and dampness will never win.

R ainbows only come with clear rain.
A ll the time it's all the same.
I wish someone would do something about it.
N othing is better than sunshine and sunlight.

Nicole Serzhantova (12)
Carmondean Primary School, Livingston

Help Us!

R ainforests are being cut down, *chop, chop, chop!*
A nimals in the rainforest are dying and becoming extinct.
I f we stop cutting down the rainforest we can see the rich
life within it.
N o rainforest is safe, so help the animals!
F rogs, crocodiles, alligators, snakes and all the other exciting
animals will die.
O pen your heart and let it all out.
R ainforests are very rare and they won't grow back.
E veryone can do their part, so you do yours.
S o keep the rainforests here
T oday and tomorrow and forever.

Brad Marcus Lambie (10)
Castlehill Primary School, Cupar

War

Some of us live in a place
Where we all get along
Where we're all friends
Where no one is at risk.

The unlucky few of us
Live in a place where
There are some stressing arguments
Or illegal happenings taking place.

But worst of all
There are the very
Unfortunate countries
Who have war.

A life of burning fire
Sickness in casualty
Can be a pleasure
To no one.

Feelings of
Anguish,
Appal,
Fear.

But unfortunately
These disasters
Are not natural
They are manmade.

It is
A big thing to stop
Maybe even
Impossible.

But if we all work together
I know
We can cease it.

Katie Phillips (10)
Castlehill Primary School, Cupar

Please Save The Homeless People

Please save the homeless people
They have nothing to do but sit on the streets.
What do they eat?
Nothing.
Save them!

Please save the homeless people
They sit on the dirty streets all day
And watch people go by
Do you know why?
They have no jobs
So they don't have any money for anything.
Save them!

Please save the homeless people
They don't have any company.
Why do they not have any company?
Because nobody talks to them.
Save them!

All I'm asking is to save them.

Could they save themselves?
Yes!
They could try to get jobs
Or save some money
Try, you can save yourself.

They can save themselves,
They could make something and sell it
And with that money
They could ask a hotel to keep them for the night.

Try!
You can save yourself
If you really try.

Fiona Simpson (9)
Castlehill Primary School, Cupar

Solution To Pollution

P ollution causes animals to die
O pen your mind to find what's right
L et us live in a clean environment
L ow pollution or no pollution is best for the world
U tter chaos will happen if we don't stop this now
T ry to find the answer in your mind
I n time if we don't stop pollution, the Earth will not survive
O n this day we must stop pollution
N o pollution is the solution!

Shane Wilson (10)
Castlehill Primary School, Cupar

War is terrible

War, war, terrible war,
Children dying,
Can you stop your unkindness,
Guns are machines
That can harm you
Very much.
Stop making explosives
For fighter jets.

Callum Edgcumbe (10)
Castlehill Primary School, Cupar

Don't Drop Litter!

L itter is not good to drop.
I n our wonderful world, litter is smelly.
T idy disgusting litter away.
T idy nasty litter into the bin.
E verything about litter is horrible.
R ecycle litter . . . put it in the bin!

Jamie Watters (10)
Castlehill Primary School, Cupar

War

War
What is the point?
War is evil,
War is bad,
One side will go home happy,
One will go home sad.
They throw a grenade, hundreds die
Why? Why? Why?
Why do they do it?
Who would want to kill?
They are trying to rule,
They charge like an angry bull
War is bad!

There was a family,
The father died.
They cried and cried and cried.
The next-door neighbour,
She was terrified with fear.
Down the road the poor boy sat
He was scared.
He knew they were coming,
Coming, coming . . .

Sean Tasker (10)
Castlehill Primary School, Cupar

Litter - Put It In The Bin

L itter is one of the things that is killing our environment.
I n the ground, on the floor pick up litter such as crisp packets
    empty sweetie wrappers, stop please!
T ip all of the smelly horrid litter into the bin.
T o save the planet put litter in the trash, that's where it belongs.
E veryone can do it, I can, so can you.
R evolting litter it's horrible, put it in the bin.

Chloe Stewart (9)
Castlehill Primary School, Cupar

Everything Deserves Respect

Animals are being treated appallingly all over the world.
Some get abandoned,
Some get shot,
Some get their habitats demolished
And now it's your turn to speak out.
Do something wonderful about it.
Let the pets have our respect
Because it's about time.

Miriam Wood (9)
Castlehill Primary School, Cupar

Pollution Senses

I feel so sad about pollution,
I see it everywhere,
I just wish I could hear it
Floating in the air.
But I can taste it
It really is not rare.
Oh the smell, it makes me want to scream!
But then I see it's 'Green Week'
And feel like I'm in a beautiful dream.

Oskar Fraser-Krauss (10)
Castlehill Primary School, Cupar

Disease

D isease is deadly
 I t can kill
S o we all need special medicine and protective shelter if we get it.
E ven if you are clean you can still catch it.
A person is dying from a terrible disease
S o we should all help them
E veryone needs help if they have a disease.

Laura Nairn (9)
Castlehill Primary School, Cupar

Animals And Extinction

All animals need attention
And fast, so they can survive.

Animals deserve a safe and happy long life.

Have they done something to us?
No, most aren't harmful, they're friendly.
They only harm us because they are afraid.

So please help the animals from extinction.
They need our *help!*

Gemma Robb (10)
Castlehill Primary School, Cupar

Litter

L ive in a clean and tidy world.
I f I can put unpleasant litter in the bin, you can!
T his huge world should be clean,
T ip the horrible litter in the bin!
E verybody can do it.
R ecycle your rubbish!

Trisha Cairney (9)
Castlehill Primary School, Cupar

Pollution

P ollution is bad for our amazing Earth.
O ne day the destroyed world is going to die.
L itter is wrong.
L et's help this lovely world, not destroy it.
U nder the muddy ground the revolting litter goes.
T here is only one way we can stop it.
I t's our responsibility to care.
O nly we can help, please!
N o pollution. Please help!

Eilidh Wood (9)
Castlehill Primary School, Cupar

War

W ars are caused by big countries fighting
and trying to get an amazing new land.
A rmies fighting, muddy bodies left to rot.
Lots of them all over the bloodstained floor.
R otting away the smelling bodies lie there.
More and more fall down and die.

Andrew Harley (9)
Castlehill Primary School, Cupar

War

W ar is killing the whole, entire planet.
A rmies killing each other. One will go on, one will not.
R evolting dead bodies lying on the ground.
No one wants to go near them.

Thomas Paterson (10)
Castlehill Primary School, Cupar

Animals

A nimals have lost their homes.
N obody should be killing the poor animals.
I nclude animals, they have feelings too.
M aybe we can make a difference
A nd please help save animals.
L osing your home is terrible.
S ave animals please!

Lori Cuthbert (9)
Castlehill Primary School, Cupar

Litter

L ift all sorts of litter up and put it in the bin.
I n shops don't drop glass bottles, you'll get fined.
T ip lots of bottles into the bin too.
T ip lots of empty cans and bottles into the bin.
E mpty crisp wrappers and others.
R ip up wrappers and put them in the bin.

Gemma Todd (10)
Castlehill Primary School, Cupar

Racism

Black or white,
You skin is alright.
Don't fight about it,
Be right about it.
If people ignore these rules,
They should be punished.
People be kind!
Our world can be a better place.
We can take one more step forward
To being better people.

Adam Scott Cook (10)
Castlehill Primary School, Cupar

Litter

L ift all the litter and put it in the bin.
I llness is caused by litter.
T rees are harmed with all our litter.
T rouble is happening with all this litter.
E very animal is eating all the litter and dying.
R ainforests are damaged by litter.

James Petrie (10)
Castlehill Primary School, Cupar

Stop War!

People dying,
Everyone crying,
All sad people.
Don't let this happen,
Everyone is so dull.

War, let it end.
War, why, why?
Families dying
It's always happening.
I hate it,
Everyone hates it.

People losing their homes,
Losing families.
Stop it!

Charlotte Hamilton (9)
Castlehill Primary School, Cupar

Rainforests

Timber, timber, timber!
Trees getting cut down as we speak.
So stop tree cutters
From taking our beautiful trees and forests.
Do they know
Amazing creatures are made homeless?
Deer, owls, hedgehogs, you name it
And they are killing them.
Save trees, from getting cut down.
Just save paper, don't waste it.
Save it!
Oh why, oh why, oh why do they do it?
Oh why?

Fionnlagh McGlashan (10)
Castlehill Primary School, Cupar

The Animal Danger

Animals looking
Left and right.
Danger lurking
In all directions.

They should be free,
Not trapped
In a damp dark cage.
Nor their lives threatened.

More and more
Lives go because of us.
Even animal lovers
Are doing it.

Help them,
Not destroy them.
Their homes
And then their lives.

We all need
To think
Do you want
Your life destroyed?

No one wants to die in pain
That is what
We are doing to them.

Life is like a baby
Just hatched.

We all need to think,
Killing animals is not a sport,
It is a crime.

Blood streams, skulls, organs
Now animals are scared of us.
It shouldn't be.
We are not looking after
Our most beautiful world.
Please help!

Caitlin Robb (10)
Castlehill Primary School, Cupar

War!

Iraq's now a wasteland,
But why is it a wasteland?
War!
War, it is a horrible thing,
War, they don't care about lives,
War, nobody can stop it,
War, it's all bad,
War, if it's so bad
Why does nobody do anything?

Ross Mitchell (11)
Cuiken Primary School, Penicuik

The Rainforest

Rainforest animals
Going through extinction
There's climate change
And felled trees
Everywhere there is pollution
Planting small trees
Makes a big difference!

Hannah Lawson (11)
Cuiken Primary School, Penicuik

Melting World

The polar bear stands on a melting world,
While cars zoom round and round.
The ice caps melt like your ice cream on a hot day
As it drips onto the ground.
So help save his ice cream
And stop him floating in a melting world.

Robert Brook (10)
Cuiken Primary School, Penicuik

Poverty

I am poor, I live on the street,
My family is dead,
I am starving and thirsty.
Every day I get weaker and weaker.
One day this lady came
She found me a home,
She found me a family,
She gave me food and water.
Every day I get stronger and stronger.
She changed a life
So why don't you?

Caitlin Dobbie (10)
Cuiken Primary School, Penicuik

Rainforests

I am feeling down,
So are other people
Because trees are getting cut down
Animals are starting to die.
So help and grow more trees to help the world
And the animals and people too.
So please help!
The wild animals in the rainforests.
Think about it,
Why cut down trees, just recycle.

Susan Greens (10)
Cuiken Primary School, Penicuik

Our Rainforest

The rainforest has been destroyed,
Animals and people evicted.
It's not for us, it's for money.
People sold off their forests
For the price of a mobile phone.
The self-centred people at the logging company
Would rather destroy their own planet than lose a few pence.
So pick up the shovel, plant a few trees
So at least you can say, 'I helped the planet breathe!'

Iain Jack Lawson (11)
Cuiken Primary School, Penicuik

How I Can Help

I heard on the TV that the rainforests were getting smaller,
Getting cut down,
But I can't help can I?
That's what I thought.
Until . . .
I found out that if I walked to school I would be cool,
Recycled when I could to make the world a better place.
I could also plant trees in our very own rainforest here in Scotland.

If I do all these things
Then I can do my best bit for the environment
Now I know how I can help.

Beth Gorrie (10)
Cuiken Primary School, Penicuik

Pollution

The animals are dying because of the air,
The world is getting polluted because of the petrol we use every day.
People without homes should get one from the government
And litter is polluting the world too.
If we recycle, we can save more trees
And replace the ones that people have cut down.
Animals lose their homes because of this.
Please do something to help!

Gemma Mack (11)
Cuiken Primary School, Penicuik

Don't Litter

Don't litter in public places, streets and towns.
Pick up litter everywhere,
Put it in the bin.
Pick up litter all around
It will make your town look good!

Matthew Garden (11)
Cuiken Primary School, Penicuik

Animal

A nimals are going extinct
N ow there are only two soft-backed turtles in one bit in China.
I n American seas there are only 5,000 bottle-nosed dolphins left.
M onkeys are going extinct, like leaf-eating monkeys.
A nimals will suddenly go if you don't help
L eopards are going extinct, there are only 4,000 left.

Please help, stop fishing with nets!

Caela Jennifer Walker (11)
Cuiken Primary School, Penicuik

Animals In Extinction

I heard on the television
That animals in Scotland
Are going extinct
Like the red squirrel
But if we plant more trees
And do not litter
These animals will get better.

Becky Graham (11)
Cuiken Primary School, Penicuik

Animals Of The World

W e will save the animals
O ver and around the world
R eptiles are going extinct
L ike all different kinds of snakes.
D o you want to save the animals of the world?

Aimie Sinton (10)
Cuiken Primary School, Penicuik

Animals And Extinction

A nimals are important.
N o litter can make a big difference.
I am disgusted at how many animals are becoming extinct.
M ost animals are extinct.
A ll animals should get noticed.
L et the world live.
S ea turtles are getting killed in nets.

Zoe Zurbriggen (10)
Cuiken Primary School, Penicuik

What Is Poverty?

Poverty is lack of food.
Poverty is just not good.
Poverty is desperation.
Poverty is bad starvation.

Poverty is when people die.
Poverty is a reason to cry.
Poverty is really that bad.
Poverty is devastatingly sad.

Poverty is when people work hard.
Poverty is when they get no reward.
Poverty is lack of money.
Poverty is so not funny.

Poverty is really unfair.
Poverty is grim; you should care!
Poverty is cruel to kids.
That's what poverty is.

Ciara Mitchell (10)
Gowriehill Primary School, Dundee

Rappin' Up War

War is wrong,
War is mean,
I'd rather be at home,
Eatin' ice cream.

If you go to war,
You could be dead,
And in the olden days
You woulda' lost your head.

Now you know,
All about war.
What I don't understand
Is what it's for.

Sam Barclay (9)
Gowriehill Primary School, Dundee

War

War,
So violent
Rockets exploding everywhere
Bombers in the sky
War.

War
Sad faces
Soldiers shooting others
Killing in the streets
War.

War
Men fighting
Corpses in buildings
Bullets spray the streets
War.

Stuart Rae (9)
Gowriehill Primary School, Dundee

Rainforest

Rainforest
nice animals
lots of animals
birds, monkeys and gorillas.
Rainforest.

Rainforest
no trees
no more animals
people destroying the forest.
Rainforest.

Sarah Georges (10)
Gowriehill Primary School, Dundee

Litterbug

When I've got the window open and I'm watching the telly,
I smell something and it's very, very smelly.
I get off my chair and look out of the window and all I can see
Is litter staring at me.

I get my coat on and walk out the door,
I run down the stairs and hear a big roar.
I walk outside and all I can see
Is rubbish shouting at me.

'Don't pick us up, please don't clean us up
We're better than your cup, please do not clean us up!'

I pick it up and keep on trying
But the litter keeps on crying
I carry on
And sing a little song.

Don't drop litter put it in
The bin!

Kelsey Mitchell (10)
Gowriehill Primary School, Dundee

Antarctica

Pollution is an atrocious thing
The ice caps are melting,
The polar bears are very scared.

The penguins are scared too.
You don't realise that, do you?
Carbon dioxide is in the air
It's running though the penguins' hair.

Graham Thomas McGee (10)
Gowriehill Primary School, Dundee

War

War
Is violence
Bombs going off
People dying also animals.
War.

War
Is horrible
Also very scary
Innocent people are dying
War.

Nicole Millar (9)
Gowriehill Primary School, Dundee

Homelessness

Helping people
Order things out
More people in the world.
Everyone always helping
Let people get shelter
Shelter can help the homeless people
Shelter keeps everybody warm and safe
Nearly loads of people pay for charity
Every single day
Shelter, shelter is the best.
Shelter, shelter helps us.

Jordan Winter (10)
Gowriehill Primary School, Dundee

Litter

L azy people drop it.
I n the bin is where it goes.
T idy if you put it in the bin
T o the bin
E arth keep it tidy
R ain will not wash it away.
        Put it in the bin!

Sarah O'Brien (10)
Gowriehill Primary School, Dundee

War

War is really sick
I really, really hate it.
Lots of people die,
It is really unpleasant.
It is so bad people die
People use rockets
I really, really hate war.
They also use bombs,
Guns, bombs, rockets, tanks, rifles.
Innocent people get hurt.

Darren Forbes (10)
Gowriehill Primary School, Dundee

War

War is violent
War is bad
War is cruel
And it makes me sad.

War is horrible
War, it sucks
I'd hate to see
Me in that muck!

Megan Charlie Grier (9)
Gowriehill Primary School, Dundee

Don't Be A Litterbug

Don't drop litter,
You might get caught.
Don't drop litter,
Or you'll get told to stop.

Use the bins that are all around,
Please turn that frown upside down.

Don't drop litter,
Crisps, sweets and banana skins.
Don't drop litter!

Lauren Scott (10)
Gowriehill Primary School, Dundee

Let's Save The Planet

R uining our planet
E co rules
C ome on, let's recycle
Y ou can do it too
C ome on, let's recycle
L et's do our bit
E ven just a bottle.

Ewan Kelly (9)
Gowriehill Primary School, Dundee

Litter

L azy litterbugs are making the world ugly.
I t is a disgrace to the world.
T errible, and more people should recycle.
T remendous when people recycle.
E nvironmentally friendly is the way to go.
R educe, reuse and recycle.

Euan Munro (9)
Halkirk Primary School, Caithness

Save The Planet

We should stop global warming to be fair,
You're saving the life of a penguin or polar bear.
Stop hunting animals that's a good thing to do,
It will be a bit greener for me and you.

Be nice to others that's a good thing to do,
Instead of killing animals and getting in trouble too.
Wars are bad - people die,
We've got to stop them that's why.

Stop pollution to be cool,
Instead walk or cycle to school.
Try and recycle that helps too,
It's best for the world - me and you.

Kirsty Robertson (10)
Halkirk Primary School, Caithness

The Poem That's Green

Walk to school, don't take the car,
It will help the atmosphere.
Do not litter
It will make the place look better.

Stop pollution,
It's unhealthy,
It could kill a penguin
Or even a polar bear.

Don't kill animals,
That could be rare
Just because you
Want their fur.

Tom Walker (10)
Halkirk Primary School, Caithness

The Green Poem

Do not litter
No more racism
No more wars
Stop pollution.

Don't hurt animals
Don't break the law
Start recycling
Walk more.

Please don't graffiti
You're destroying our surroundings
And the world I care about
I hope that you do too.

Bryony MacDonald (10)
Halkirk Primary School, Caithness

Rainforest Destruction

R ainforests with lots of species
A nd everything being cut down
I n such a horrid state
N o one seems to care
F or our glorious rainforest
O r the beautiful animals
R oaring fire sweeps the land
E ating up habitats in its path
S tealing through the rainforest
T aking rare species and selling them as pets
S o let's save rainforests!

Charlie Innes (9)
Halkirk Primary School, Caithness

Poverty

Famine and drought,
People starving, living in doubt.
No clean water from wells
People are suffering, can't you tell?

Do you think they're happy?
No school, no toys.
Do you think they're happy?
Those girls and boys.

We take things for granted
Like water, food and light.
They don't have them,
So try to help them out.

Bryony-Skye Sanderson (10)
Halkirk Primary School, Caithness

Save The Earth

To stop the wars
You've got to stop the racism.
To save the Earth
We should all get along.

To save the animals
You've got to stop the hunters.
To save the Earth
We need lots of species.

To stop global warming
You've got to stop pollution.
To save the Earth
We must look after it now!

Matthew Cowan (11)
Halkirk Primary School, Caithness

The Environment

People are destroying the environment
So I have to ask why?
Why do they cut down trees and plants?
We need to eat plants too.
Turn off taps and have a shower
But don't stay in it for an hour.

Recycling will help us stop wasting things
Like glass, metal and wood.
It's really fun and keeps you busy
And also it's very good.
Never over-fish for sharks and whales
Don't watch too much TV and don't keep watching Emmerdale.

I know three things you should never do,
Stand up and I'll give you a clue.
One is letting your weeds overgrow
Definitely don't use your car for no reason
You can easily walk.
Another thing is turn off the taps and lights
You'll also save energy.

Jennifer Don (10)
Halkirk Primary School, Caithness

Animals In Danger

E xtinction can happen
N ever to be seen again
D ead forever
A nimals lose habitats
N o more food for them to eat
G reat innocent animals are dying
E very day it happens
R eally it's upsetting
E ndangered animals are coming to an end
D o something about it.

Jessica Florence (9)
Halkirk Primary School, Caithness

Saving The Planet

Don't hunt to kill,
You might get fined with a big bill.
Only hunt for food,
That would be good.

Don't call people black,
You might get a whack.
No more fighting
It's very frightening.

Don't hurt people
And don't vandalise the church steeple.
That would be bad
And it would make the vicar mad.

Euan Bremner (10)
Halkirk Primary School, Caithness

How To Save Energy

To save energy you . . .
Cycle to school,
Recycle to be cool,
Instead of being a fool.

You can make the world
A better place by . . .
Turning off lights
And saving memory bites.

If you want to save energy
You can start right now.
You could save the world
And the future. *Wow! Wow!*

Ian Mackay (10)
Halkirk Primary School, Caithness

Young Writers - The Big Green Poetry Machine Scotland Poets

Global Warming - Haiku

Ice caps melting fast
Polar bears are dying out
The seas are rising.

Katie Macleod (9)
Halkirk Primary School, Caithness

War!

What a sight people saw
What a fight people saw
As people died
And people saw
Realising it was because
War!

Brandon Brinded (10)
Halkirk Primary School, Caithness

Can We Save Earth?

Something is wrong
I can't hear the birds anymore
Something is wrong.
Why can't I hear their pretty song
The horrible things I saw
I don't want to see anymore
Something is wrong.

Isla Louise Cartwright (10)
Halkirk Primary School, Caithness

Save The Rainforest

R eady to stop trees being cut down?
A mazon Basin in South America has one fifth
of the world's oxygen.
I n years to come, trees will be no more!
N ow be an eco-freak.
F or our world's sake, stop cutting down trees.
O nly we can save the world.
R ights for not cutting down trees.
E xtinction for animals like the orang-utan.
S tart and change the world.
T ime to make a stand.
S top it now!

Christopher Gunn (10)
Halkirk Primary School, Caithness

Pollution

P olluting the air
O n the streets there's always litter
L and getting destroyed by pollution
L aziness by Man
U se recycling bins
T ry to save our planet
I nvolve people in recycling
O ur world needs your help
N ever throw litter round streets.

Andrew David McLaren (10)
Halkirk Primary School, Caithness

Litter - Haikus

Litter is a crime,
It kills lots of animals,
It should be stopped now.

Litter is nasty,
It wrecks the environment,
It should be banned now.

Litter is awful,
It is harmful to the world
It should be finished.

Erin Shearsmith (9)
Halkirk Primary School, Caithness

Litter

L oads of people throw wrappers into the sea and on the ground.
I t is our environment that is getting damaged.
T he feeling you get is guilt.
T he litter you throw is bad.
E veryone can pitch in and recycle!
R ecycling can make the world a better place.

Jack McKee (9)
Halkirk Primary School, Caithness

Litterbugs

L ess people are helping the environment
I n countries, cities and towns!
T aking over the green field sites
T he landfills are filling up
E very day litter is dropped
R ivers, seas and lakes are getting polluted.
        Please help!

Terri Liz Munro (8)
Halkirk Primary School, Caithness

Animal Extinction - Haiku

Animals fly by
They are endangered mammals
And they will die soon.

Louise Fraser (9)
Halkirk Primary School, Caithness

War

R acing into war
A nd people hurt badly.
C hildren fighting with a bar
I njured people lying sadly.
S o many ambulances racing by
M ore people sigh.

Declan Gunn (9)
Halkirk Primary School, Caithness

What Goes On

Things are happening
Animals are dying out
By Man's mad machines.

L ess people are helping the environment
I n countries and towns they aren't helping
T he pandas are dying by Man
T he landfills are filling up more
E co-people can help us
R ivers and seas are being polluted.

Craig Kennedy Yuille (9)
Halkirk Primary School, Caithness

War - Haiku

Fierce fighting kills
In lots of different countries
Let-down children cry.

Lewis Sutherland (9)
Halkirk Primary School, Caithness

Litter

L itter is bad for nature.
I want the environment to be saved.
T he world is dying because of us!
T hings should not be thrown on the street.
E nvironmentalists are trying to save the world.
R ecycle your rubbish before it's too late.

Jamie Mackay (10)
Halkirk Primary School, Caithness

Don't Drop Litter!

L itter is getting dropped everywhere. It should stop.
I n the water fish are getting caught in ring pulls. Stop!
T errible schoolchildren are dropping litter. It should stop now.
T ragic people are not putting litter in the bin. Help the environment.
E nvironment is not doing very well. We should put up more signs.
R ing pulls are getting caught in animals' throats. Don't do that!

Shaun Gunn (9)
Halkirk Primary School, Caithness

Animals

A llow animals to live
N ever kill a healthy animal
I vory is not for poaching or selling
M an is selfish
A nimals heading for extinction
L ives are being lost
S ave our environment now!

Scott Yuille (9)
Halkirk Primary School, Caithness

The Litterbugs

L andfill sites are taking over the world
I n the ocean fish are getting killed
T errible litter has been dropped in the sea
T owns are getting covered in litter
E arth is getting covered in litter
R educe, reuse, recycle!

Charlie Firth (9)
Halkirk Primary School, Caithness

Litter

L oads of litter about
I t is very bad for you
T ime to sort it all out
T o help the environment
E nergy is getting wasted all the time
R emember to recycle and save energy.

Skye Rogerson (9)
Halkirk Primary School, Caithness

Making The World A Better Place

To make the world a better place,
Recycle things and use them again.
Walk to places, don't take the car,
Stop racism it's not a laugh.

Don't break the law,
Do not hunt,
Animals are endangered,
So don't kill them.

Stop pollution,
Don't hurt others,
No more wars,
You're killing others,
It's not nice.

Emma Coghill (10)
Halkirk Primary School, Caithness

How To Make The World
A Better Place

Do not litter,
Do not fight!
Stop pollution
And do not hunt!

Don't break the law
And don't start wars.
Don't be a racist
And don't aid global warming!

Walk more,
Look after your health.
Don't do graffiti
And do not waste energy!

James Barry Brotherston (11)
Halkirk Primary School, Caithness

The Environment

Saving energy is so cool
When it comes to doing it in school.
If we don't react right now
The world will be polluted!

Draining energy is not nice
And penguins will have no more ice.
When you're cold put a jumper on
And don't turn on your heating.

When it's bright
Turn off your lights
And if it's nice, cycle to school
And don't use your car.

Why don't you be a part of the Big Green Team
And try to help save the environment?

Megan Mackay (10)
Halkirk Primary School, Caithness

Saving The Earth

Don't litter, if you look there are bins everywhere.
Help global warming and pollution.
Just from turning a switch off,
You could maybe save the Earth.
Walk to school you could be much healthier
And save fuel by not using the car.
Useless electricity, use renewable energy.
So think and maybe you could save the *Earth!*

Elly Jackson (10)
Halkirk Primary School, Caithness

Litter

L itter should be banned because it kills nature.
I want to save the environment.
T o save the animals, you've got to tell people they're in danger.
T hings should not be thrown on the streets.
E nvironmentalists are trying to save the world.
R ubbish should be put in a recycling bin.

James Alexander Mackintosh (8)
Halkirk Primary School, Caithness

I'm Just A Little Can

I'm an aluminium can, small and round
But please don't think about chucking me on the ground.
Don't throw me against the wall
Or use me to play football.
I'm just a little empty tin
I'm not meant for the rubbish bin.
You wouldn't think I had that much power
But recycling me can run a TV for three hours!

Bryan Rennie (11)
Hill Primary School, Blairgowrie

Reduce, Reuse And Recycle!

I'm a sheet of paper, don't put me in the rubbish bin
If you do you're killing trees, that really is a sin.
Please don't pop me in the rubbish bin or you will regret it
Put me in the recycling bin, you'll help the Earth a bit.
If you use both sides of me
You'll help more than just one tree.
So next time you use paper, remember what we say
The three golden rules that help us every day,
Reduce, reuse and recycle
OK!

Heather Smith (11)
Hill Primary School, Blairgowrie

Recycle That Bottle

I am a glass bottle, empty, small and thin
But what are you going to do to me,
Chuck me in the bin?
I want to have another life, so please recycle me
The landfill sites are filling up,
Just look and you will see . . .

Those mountains are for real, there's rubbish all around
They reach up to the sky from way down in the ground
The soil is polluted, the clay, the dust, the sand
The landfill sites are filling and taking over the land

You can help all this you know, you can help it stop
Just pop me in the recycling bin next time you're at the shop!

Alison Rae (11)
Hill Primary School, Blairgowrie

The Plastic Bag

I'm a plastic bag you see,
From a big brand company.
I'm blowing round and round the street,
Trampled on by many feet.
You thought you could get rid of me,
But now I'm making history!
Killing off the local wildlife,
Causing trouble, causing strife!
If you throw me in the bin,
You are committing another sin.
But if you think to recycle me,
You'll find many will be happy.
I'll be made into many things,
A new work surface? Plastic rings?
So do not leave me on the ground,
If you want to keep the environment safe and sound!

Briana Freed Smith (12)
Hill Primary School, Blairgowrie

It's A Battery's Life

I am a battery, use me if you dare
But when you're ready to throw me out, think and beware.
Forty-one million of me are sent to landfill sites each year
And when my poisonous insides spill out, you'll be the one in fear.
They will poison the soil, ruining all in sight
And unfortunately, it isn't something you can fight.
But there is another option, to save you from the worry
Of rushing to find a new home in a hurry.
Recycle me at the supermarket, in the battery bin
Then you can walk off happily with a proud grin.

Caitlin Mackenzie (11)
Hill Primary School, Blairgowrie

I Am A Glass Bottle

I am a glass bottle made of sand, limestone and salt;
Because you put me in the bin it's all your fault.
I'll end up in a landfill site,
You should have recycled me. You must know that is right!
So recycle me now!
You might be thinking *how?*
Well drop me off at the recycling place,
They'll recycle me at a slow, steady pace.
You can run a television for an hour by recycling me
And my life can begin again. *Yippee!*

James Clarkson (11)
Hill Primary School, Blairgowrie

The Battery
That Wants Another Chance

I'm a little battery,
Full of lots of energy,
But when I'm finished,
I can be replenished.
If you let me die,
I'll make the planet cry.
Recharge or recycle me,
I can be reused you see.
Most supermarkets have a battery bin,
That's where you should pop me in.
The landfill sites are getting full,
Recycling is cool!

Daniel Duncan (11)
Hill Primary School, Blairgowrie

Extinction

The ice is melting,
The penguins have nowhere to go.

Elephants have been hunted and many tigers too,
Now the only safe place for them, is in a zoo.

A lot of the monkeys in the trees,
Are facing the problem of disease.

Ben Black (10)
Iona Primary School, Argyll

Recycling

R ecycling is a good thing to do,
E verybody save our planet,
C an you help us please?
Y ou should have a recycling bin at home.
C an you help people recycle?
L ittering is bad,
I t is bad to throw rubbish away.
N obody should throw rubbish away.
G et out of your car and start walking to school.

Zoe Graham (8)
Kinglassie Primary School, Kinglassie

Rainforest

R emember to switch the TV off
A nimals are in danger because of pollution
I want to save the planet
N ever leave your car on
F orests are being cut down
O ceans are getting polluted with rubbish
R emember to switch your computer off
E veryone should recycle
S ave our planet
T ell everyone to help save the planet!

Chelsea Leigh Hutchison (8)
Kinglassie Primary School, Kinglassie

Pollution

P ollution is bad for our planet,
O ceans are full of oil,
L itter is bad for our planet,
L ots of litter is in the oceans,
U se recycling bins,
T urn off your lights and TVs
I t's time to save the world,
O rang-utans are endangered,
N atural disasters are stopping today.

Craig Harlow (8)
Kinglassie Primary School, Kinglassie

Rainforest

R ecycle cans and paper,
A nimals are endangered,
I n our homes recycle,
N othing can stop you helping the world,
F orests are getting cut down for paper,
O ceans are getting destroyed from litter,
R ecycle your milk cartons, paper, cans and cards.
E veryone help the world and recycle.
S et endangerd animals free.
T Vs should not be on standby all the time, switch
off at the switch.

Lauren Paterson (9)
Kinglassie Primary School, Kinglassie

Rainforest

R ecycle your paper and cans,
A nimals are endangered,
I n our world we care for animals,
N o one should be littering,
F orests are getting cut down and animals are losing their habitats,
O rang-utans are endangered because people are keeping
them as pets,
R ainforest animals are endangered,
E xtinction is not far away from us,
S et endangered animals free,
T Vs should not be left on standby.

Ceira Knox (9)
Kinglassie Primary School, Kinglassie

Rainforest

R ainforests are getting destroyed for paper.
A nimals are getting hunted for their fur.
I walk to school.
N ever drop litter.
F orests are getting cut down.
O ceans have got too much litter in them.
R hinoceros are getting killed for their horns.
E veryone save the world!
S ave the poor people!
T rees are getting cut down for paper.

Euan Watters (8)
Kinglassie Primary School, Kinglassie

Litter

L itter is so bad
I don't like litter on the ground.
T rees are being destroyed.
T oucans have a funny name.
E xterminate litter.
R ecycle litter.

William Pirrie (8)
Kinglassie Primary School, Kinglassie

Recycle

Rainforest animals in danger,
Extinction is not far away from us,
Coke cans pollute as well.
You can make a difference,
Life is harder than you think,
Everyone look after our planet!

Simone Sallan (9)
Kinglassie Primary School, Kinglassie

Litter

L ike our world and don't leave litter,
I don't like our world because it is not clean.
T rees help us breathe so don't cut them down.
T ry to save the planet.
E veryone make this world clean.
R ecycle paper please!

Emma Fotheringham (8)
Kinglassie Primary School, Kinglassie

Litter

L itter is bad for our planet.
I don't drop litter.
T he world gets polluted every second.
T he world is a sphere.
E very year the world dies.
R ainforest animals are endangered.

Liam James Gay (9)
Kinglassie Primary School, Kinglassie

You Can Help

Please recycle rubbish,
Try to save the world,
Do not use a car to travel to school,
Birds are dying from pollution,
You can help, all you need to do is
Put rubbish in a bin!
Try to save the rainforest and the world!
You can help!

Taylor Thomson (8)
Kinglassie Primary School, Kinglassie

Rainforest

R emember to turn your TV off.
A nimals are under threat because people are killing them.
I want to save the planet.
N ever drop litter.
F orests are getting destroyed.
O ceans sometimes have pollution in the water.
R ecycle all your paper.
E veryone look after animals.
S ave the planet.
T urn off the computer!

Kali Wright (8)
Kinglassie Primary School, Kinglassie

Rainforest

R emember to recycle,
A nimals are in danger,
I will help animals.
N o one should be a litterbug,
F orests are getting destroyed,
O ceans are full of pollution,
R ecycle everything,
E veryone should stop destroying the habitats,
S ave our planet,
T ell people to stop hunting animals.

Breagha Kipling (9)
Kinglassie Primary School, Kinglassie

Litter

Litter, litter is the worst
Or all the money in your purse.

Don't drop your litter please
Or I will come and bite your knees.

So tidy up your litter, it's really, really easy,
Come on you can help us, it's really easy-peasy!

Save the planet!

Rachel Carr (9)
Kinglassie Primary School, Kinglassie

Recycling

R ecycle
E nergy
C lean the world
Y ou can help clean up the rubbish
C ycling is great
L eave the car at home, it's not very far
I t is really good to recycle
N ow we are making the world a better place
G ive up the car.

Argyll McCoist (9)
Langbank Primary School, Langbank

Recycling Litter

R ecycling
E verything will
C lean up the mess
Y ou can help if you don't put it in the bin
C lear all the rubbish
L et the world be clean
I f you don't help us
N ow trees will still be
G reen.

Max Ashmore (9)
Langbank Primary School, Langbank

Racism Reject

R acism is a disgrace.
A cross the whole wide world,
C ausing it to hurt people's feelings,
I s it affecting you?
S tay strong and keep your head up high.
M en and women!

Marisa Diane Keegan (9)
Langbank Primary School, Langbank

The Sixth Sense

Every day I hear the thwack of axes against trees,
The crunch of the bark as oaks topple down.
Every day I see litter crawling across the road,
Animals caught in cans and bags.
Paper will decompose but bottles take years.
Every day I smell pollution, dying creatures in the sea.
What will happen if they disappear?
Every day I feel war, suffering people, women, men and children.
Bombs raining down on buildings and cars, when will it end?
Every day I smell extinction, porpoises, elephants and tigers,
Soon there will be none left; what will they do?
I have a sixth sense, it is for the environment
I wonder if wars will end, pollution will black out,
Extinction will go dim.
Every day I use my sixth sense.

Ross Eaglesham (9)
Langbank Primary School, Langbank

Rainforest

R ainforests are being destroyed
A nimals could be gone by the time we die
I f we do nothing
N o more pollution to kill the planet
F or all is living
O r nothing could be living - decide
R ight now is when you
E nd this pollution
S o stop polluting
T oday is when you decide.

Ross Tyre (9)
Langbank Primary School, Langbank

Rainforest

Jaguars creep up on their prey
Parrots squeal when they think they are in trouble
Monkeys run when they hear the parrots cry
Run, run, run, run from the jaguar
Bats go out at night in the rainforest.

Ants clear up most of the place, like rotting fruit, leaves and lots more
Snakes kill their enemies to eat them
Caterpillars crunch in the rainforest.

They cut down trees so they can make furniture and to build houses.

People in the rainforest are called Indians.

Katie Joss (7)
Longforgan Primary School, Longforgan

Rainforest

Ants creep through the rainforest to clean it up.
Jaguars prowl through the canopy, the parrots scream for help.
Bromeliads up in the canopy, frogs jump in the water, *plop!*
Crocodiles cruise, watching and they pounce.
If a tree is dead the ants come and clean it up very quickly.
Stilted houses are in a quiet village.

Gavin Anderson (7)
Longforgan Primary School, Longforgan

Rainforest

Jaguars hunt their prey,
Up in the canopy parrots cry.
Jaguars go to attack,
Parrots scream - and the monkeys grab their babies
And run for their lives.
Snakes kill other animals. A tree frog waits for a fly.
Monkeys swing from tree to tree.

Dylan Reid (8)
Longforgan Primary School, Longforgan

Rushing, Gurgling Water

Ants cleaning up the rainforest, picking up fruit.
Indians hunting for food.
Native plants are catching rain.
Flying butterflies are flying around in the understory.
Orang-utans are swinging from tree to tree.
Jumping jaguars are hunting for food.
Animals are hunting their food.
Sloths are moving so slowly.
Trees are giving oxygen.

Lewis Hunter (7)
Longforgan Primary School, Longforgan

My Rainforest Poem

Monkeys swing from tree to tree,
Jaguars hunt in the canopy.
The sloth hangs upside down,
Ants crawl along the forest floor.
Butterflies flying around,
Boa constrictors stay on the ground.

Beth McNeish (8)
Longforgan Primary School, Longforgan

The Rainforest

R ainforests have lots of animals and lots of bugs too.
A nts clear up and make a good job.
I t rains a lot in the rainforest.
N ice small animals in the rainforest.
F lying through the trees is a flying squirrel.
O val-shaped leaves fall from trees.
R unning up the trees, a jaguar.
E very day things swing from tree to tree.
S inging parrots in the trees.
T he rainforest is a quiet place.

Ben Dunmore (8)
Longforgan Primary School, Longforgan

Running Through The Rainforest

R ushing through the rainforest
A nimals screech and jaguars seeking
I t's dark in the rainforest
N o sun gets in
F ishes spend their time in water
O f all the animals they have different noises
R uined because of people
E very animal walks with different moves
S nakes come from the Amazon
T igers have orange and black fur.

Adam Cartwright (8)
Longforgan Primary School, Longforgan

Rainforest

The parrots are squeaking
The monkeys are running
The rain is rushing
Jaguars climb the trees
Jaguars jump on their prey

Flies' food is smelly, disgusting meat
It is soggy and wet and squelchy
You can hear *ooh, ooh, ooh, ah, ah, ah*
And screaming!

Natalie McKinnie (7)
Longforgan Primary School, Longforgan

The Rainforest

Rainforest is great to learn about
Crocodile, bushbaby and ring-tailed lemur
Rainforest is great to learn about.

Snake, sloth and monkey
Rainforest is great to learn about
Gorilla, bat and parrot
Rainforest is great to learn about.

Leopard and tiger
Rainforest is great to learn about
Frog, eagle and ant
Rainforest is great to learn about.

Charlotte Jennings (8)
Longforgan Primary School, Longforgan

Jaguar

Jaguar always jumping
Jaguar always pouncing
The rain always drips on the jaguar
Jaguar always wet
Jaguar always hot
Jaguar always jumping, jumping too
Jaguar sometimes sleeping.

Cameron Johnston (7)
Longforgan Primary School, Longforgan

Rainforest Poem

Monkeys swing from tree to tree
Parrots flap in the canopy
Anteaters lick at the ground
Jaguars pounce and pound
Sloths go as slow as snails
One of them has a long nail
Capybaras scrunch up all the leaves
One of them thinks that ants are thieves
But last of all my favourite one
The lemur who has lots of fun.

Abby Lang (8)
Longforgan Primary School, Longforgan

My Poem

R unning through the trees
A nimals jumping from tree to tree
I n the trees parrots hide
N aughty jaguars jump up and down
F rom tree to tree monkeys swing around the rainforest
O ut and about there are animals to see
R eptiles are everywhere
E veryone can see
S loths swing from tree to tree
T igers jump up and down all the way around the rainforest.

Jamie Dunmore (8)
Longforgan Primary School, Longforgan

Litter

L itter is bitter
I know what to do
T ry and help
T ime to stop littering
E verybody can do it
R ecycle your stuff that you don't need.

Susie Garratt (8)
New Aberdour School, Fraserburgh

Rare Animals

All animals big and small
All animals skinny and tall.
Dodos are rare, so is a polar bear
I'd beware if you dare.
Some are purple including a turtle.
Some are white including albino.

Heather Perkins (9)
New Aberdour School, Fraserburgh

Recycle

R ecycle to make the world a better place
E veryone get your scrap out
C an you help us?
Y ou can save the world
C ans, card and glass can be recycled
L itter is bitter
E arth needs your help.

Ryan Borwick (8)
New Aberdour School, Fraserburgh

Young Writers - The Big Green Poetry Machine Scotland Poets

Make The Difference

Today is nothing different,
Today is nothing new.
No one can change today
Apart from me and you.

The days are getting warmer,
It might sound good to us
But in the Arctic
It's causing quite a fuss.

The Arctic is a special place,
But the ice is melting away.
So the ice that was the Arctic
Could be gone by May.

The Arctic has some cool creatures
Including the polar bear
But they will be gone
If we don't show them some care.

Tomorrow think of them
Or there will come a dawn
When all rare animals
Will be gone.

So instead of taking lots of baths,
For once have a shower.
Believe me,
It will use less power.

Dana Leslie (10)
Park Place Primary School, Dundee

Help The Homeless

Help the homeless
Over the years
More people have become
Less fortunate than us.
Every day they are trying to earn money.
Save the homeless, help them have a nice life.
Save the homeless, you could make a difference to the world.

Eden Miller (9)
Park Place Primary School, Dundee

Earth Day

The stars shine like crystals on a sunny day.
Earth is round as a cat's eye marble.
Clouds fly gently in the sky.
Waters blue with animals beautiful and new.
Land has many wonders and lots to behold.

An island covered in green trees with green grass and green leaves.
Buildings stand in the bright light.
The sky lies on the horizon waiting for night.
Mountains so high almost touch the sky.
Hills and valleys with the sun rise.

Snowy glitter lands melt into sea.
Starving children scream, 'Please help me!'
Little child tries to ride in water.
Factories make the world go hotter.
The air is poisoned spitting out more than ever.

The Earth screams in pain and agony, 'Help, please!'

Rebecca Greig (11)
Ravenscraig Primary School, Inverclyde

Earth Day

Shining stars sparkle like candle lights around Planet Earth
Crystal-blue oceans reflect the sun's golden rays
Puffy little clouds float softly above the cold air

Rugged mountains standing tall and still
Blankets of green trees swaying in the crisp air
Sparkly pale buildings gaze at the blue seas
Stunning skies shine on the horizon.

Crystal ice caps melt gradually into growing seas
A slim zebra lies thirsty on the red burnt land
Factories fire out disgusting smoke
While people strain through flooding streets
Planet Earth squeals, 'It's not too late, please save me!'

Ellis Cunningham (10)
Ravenscraig Primary School, Inverclyde

Earth Day

Bright stars shine like Christmas lights on Planet Earth
There oceans are crystal-blue when the sun makes it golden
Lovely floating white clouds move above like a beautiful rabbit
That holds many wonders.
The Rocky Mountains standing tall
Green trees swaying in the soft breeze
Sapphire skies float on the horizon seas
White sparkling buildings look out at the soft empty seas

Snowy polar ice caps melt slowly into rising seas
And no water
People struggle through flooded streets

Choking smoke surrounding factories in cities
The planet cries out, 'Help me please!'

Kiera Purdie (10)
Ravenscraig Primary School, Inverclyde

Earth Day

The stars surround the Earth, burning like candles
A blue marble in their ring
Flowing ocean waves glimmer as they reflect the white blur
Of the moon,
Just like a crystal
Shining cotton hovers over seas of sapphire
Which shield a distant land that seems lifeless . . .
From a view in space.

Mountains look over a small seashore town
Of white buildings
A pale scarlet sky meets a vast stretch
Of gleaming water on the horizon
To reflect on the shimmering waves
The coastline, home to a blanket
Of lime-green trees,
Positioned boldly on the thin, sandy ledge.

The polar ice caps melt ever so slowly
Into menacing black water, so deep, so freezing . . .
While another country is being baked under the sun,
Red soil exposed to the orange ball
Animals drop with dehydration
And people struggle through famine-stricken lands
Pollution spreads and swollen seas rise into floods.

Sinking in distress, Planet Earth bellows out,
'I'm heating up! Make an effort and cool me down!'

Laura Fulton (10)
Ravenscraig Primary School, Inverclyde

Earth Day

Shining stars look upon the Earth at night
The ocean swerves as the sun looks down at it
Puffy clouds fly gently above a lot of lovely landscapes
The sun shines all over the world and makes it bright

Bright white buildings watch the sea
Trees are moving when the gasp of wind hits them
The sky floats over the sparkling horizon
Mountains stand tall all day

Melting polar caps disappear very slowly
Animals die from dehydration
Families evacuate their house from the floods
Cars and factories pollute the Earth all day
Help the planet as it screeches out, 'Please, please save me!'

Robyn McGhee (10)
Ravenscraig Primary School, Inverclyde

Earth Day

Stars shine like crystals
On the Earth creating light
Sapphire oceans reflect the sun's golden rays
Clouds like snow float smoothly above a land
That is full of wonder and light
Mountains' position rugged and tall
Sheets of trees sway gently in the breeze
Rows of buildings glance out onto the empty seas
Skies float on the distant horizon
Snowy polar caps slowly disappear into the rising seas
Working factories pollute the air with ghastly smoke
A shrivelled ox lies on burning red sand
Rising seas, like a running tap, create floods all around
Causing people trouble

The planet wails, *'It's not too late!'*

Beth MacGugan (10)
Ravenscraig Primary School, Inverclyde

Earth Day

Bright stars shine like Christmas lights on planet Earth
The seas swaying from side to side
The land beautiful green like green, green grass
Rocky mountains standing tall
Tall buildings gazing out to seas
Blankets of green trees swaying in the gentle breeze
Snowy, soft, polar ice caps melting very slowly
A cow's skeleton lies on boiling sandy soil
People struggling to get through flooded land
Factories exploding out choking smoke
Our world cries out, *'Save us!'* It's *not* too late!'

Ashleigh McCready (10)
Ravenscraig Primary School, Inverclyde

Earth

Shining stars glow like the moon around our planet
Its cool blue waters surround the emerald-green lands
And the crystal, pale, blue skies skirt the fluffy clouds
That float gently through the air

Rocky mountains stand tall and still
Green trees look like blankets covering the lands
And the brick buildings stare out at the motionless sapphire seas

White polar caps melt slowly into rising seas
Thousands drown in terrible floods that wash away
Hopes and dreams
Factories release black choking smoke that kills and pollutes
And the dry, sandy lands grow skeletal animals that lie motionless

The planet wails, 'Save me! Please help! It's not too late!'

Sophie Hunter (10)
Ravenscraig Primary School, Inverclyde

Earth Day

Shiny stars sparkle like candles around the planet
Puffy white clouds float along softly on thin air
The different colours of sea shine and sparkle in the darkness

The pointy mountains stand tall in the sky
White buildings stare out to the deep blue sea
A longboat cruises gently along the sea
A single tiny island stands in the middle of the water, lonely

The smoke blows out like a train
The people start to become ill and unhealthy
The dirty black water floods the town making people's lives a misery

'Help! Stop it now!' screams the Earth!

Rebecca Quinn (10)
Ravenscraig Primary School, Inverclyde

Alone

I live on the streets
It's dirty and cold
Please listen to my story
It has to be told
I have no home to call my own
I beg and borrow
And feel only sorrow
Please read my poem
Then, maybe, one day
My luck will change
And I won't be homeless
And sleep in the rain.
Maybe, just maybe, together
We can break this chain.

Morgan McLatchie (7)
St Gabriel's RC Primary School, Greenock

Litter

Do not throw litter on the ground
The litter will blow around.
The litter will make a mess
And the place wants to look its best.
It might only be a small pollution
But we have to find a big solution.
So stop, think for a minute
Don't drop it, go bin it!

Cara Turner (6)
St Gabriel's RC Primary School, Greenock

The Rainforest

In the rainforest if you look up high,
You'll see the trees that touch the sky,
Their big canopy will cover the ground,
So if you look down few plants will be found,
The weather is moist, humid and hot,
A cold drink of water, will really hit the spot,
If you go to a rainforest you'll see what I mean,
When you come back, you'll love what you've seen.

Jennifer Gray (7)
St Gabriel's RC Primary School, Greenock

How Recycling Can Be Fun

R ecycling can be fun
E veryone can join in
C ome on and take a chance
Y ou can make a difference
C hildren and adults too
L earn to recycle
E nvironment will then be safer for you.

Amie Louise Martin (9)
St Monica's Primary School, Kirkwood

The Battle Against War

War, war it's just a kick and scratch
You wouldn't see that in a football match
It's just two countries fighting to see who's the best
They're wrecking the planet for all the rest.

Let's all stand up
Against war we will fight
Who believes in war?
It's just not right!

I can't believe people love to fight
It's just a really disgraceful sight
Let's say, 'No!' to war
Goodbye and goodnight.

Aiden Ward (11)
St Monica's Primary School, Kirkwood

Keep The World Colourful

I like the world it's so cool, it's my favourite place to be.
But there's pollution, death and war and people cutting down trees.
Racism is another point. The person's the same as you.
They're only a different colour or race, have glasses or
                                             different shoes.
Litterbugs annoy me. They could put their rubbish in the bin
Or they could help the world a bit by recycling.
The sky is blue, the grass is green. I want it to stay that way.
But with all the global warming, that could change any day.
Everyone can help the world no matter what colour or race.
Everyone, become an eco-kid and make the world a better place.

I like bright colours, I like loomy. I never like dull.
Everyone help the world and it will always be colourful.

Amy McSwiggan (11)
St Monica's Primary School, Kirkwood

Reality Of It

There's litter at my feet,
As I walk down the street,
Look at the litter over there,
Please pick it up even if you don't care.

Recycle your bits and bobs
Do you know that's some people's jobs?
We can make it new again
Do you hear what I'm saying?

Litter, litter, you smell so bad
And you make me feel sad
To see our streets covered in rubbish
If you leave I will shoosh!

Rhiannon McEnroe (11)
St Monica's Primary School, Kirkwood

Rampant Recyclers

Recycling is really the thing to do,
Whether it's old clothes or a bottle or two.
When you use paper you are destroying the trees,
So recycle the paper, I'm begging you, please!

We could make pencils from anything but trees,
Maybe from the cases of old CDs.
If you recycle, it would mean a lot,
And if you don't, I'll cook you in a pot!

I'm just kidding, it's only a joke,
Now go recycle your sweetie poke.

Joseph Brannigan (11)
St Monica's Primary School, Kirkwood

Litter, Litter Go Away

Litter, litter go away,
Don't come back any day,
Litter smells, litter reeks,
Stay away from the streets.

I can see some trash bins,
And still I see litter everywhere,
Why don't people use the bins
And not be such a pear?

Darren Conway (11)
St Monica's Primary School, Kirkwood

We Should All Be Friends

Don't pick on someone
Because they are not the same
Be nice to them
Let them join in your game.

If you are doing this
You are a bully and no more
If you come near me
I'll show you the door.

Regardless of the colour
That you are
Everyone in this world
Is a star.

It doesn't matter
What religion we attend
God made us
To all be friends.

All over the world
There are different places
Who cares where you come from?
We should all have smiles on our faces!

Elysha McLaughlin (11)
St Monica's Primary School, Kirkwood

Litter, Litter, Litter

Oh, this world is a state,
With all the mess that we create.
The litter flies around the town,
It makes us sad and then we frown.
Oh dear Lord, help this be
A better world for You and me.

I wish you'd put your litter in the bin,
And if you do, it's you that'll win.
What it is I'm trying to say,
Is keep your litter far away.
We don't want anything to do with litter,
Because we want the best place
And not the bitter.

Jodie Hetherston (11)
St Monica's Primary School, Kirkwood

Litterbugs

The world is full of plastic bags
And litter,
Over the streets they go,
Crisp packets and lots, lots more.

These are the things
That are hurting our planet.
We are the ones . . .
Who make the mess,
The litterbugs,
Oh no, no, no!

Next time you have a packet of crisps,
Find a wheelie bin.

We are the only ones
Who can stop this dreadful thing!

Kiera Cullen (11)
St Monica's Primary School, Kirkwood

Scarred For Life

The terror came out from the sky
Or so we're led to think.
With gas and guns and aeroplane bombs
The world was on the brink.

But the government, it had a plan
You see there was oil beneath the sand
It would start a war on terror
And liberate those lands.

So we watched as the propaganda started
And believed every line we were fed
And off to war our boys went
We're still burying the dead.

So as the years have passed
Are we any better off?
Our brothers are still dying
But ask yourself, for what?

So when you go to sleep tonight
In your warm and cosy bed
Spare a thought for the deserts
That are littered with the dead!

Aiden Mackinnon (9)
St Monica's Primary School, Kirkwood

Litter

Please don't drop your litter or people will be sad.
When they see you doing it they will say, 'That boy is bad!'
If you put it in the bin, you shall see people with a grin.
So please don't drop your litter because it is a disgrace.
Please make the town you live in a much better place.
It might blow into a farm and make an animal hurt.
So please don't drop your litter or your town will look like dirt.

Taylor McAllister (11)
St Monica's Primary School, Kirkwood

Big Green Recycle Machine

Big green recycle machine
Gobble up all the litter
Don't take the car, for global warming
Plus you'll get even fitter
Racism is in someone's life
In most poor countries it is rife
Animals and extinction too!
Imagine if that animal were you!
Rainforest animals are losing their homes
And will be left somewhere
Somewhere alone!
Help the world get better
Let us see
A beautiful world
For you and me!

Beckie McEwan (12)
St Monica's Primary School, Kirkwood

Racism Hurts

Racism hurts, it isn't right
It gets you into a lot of fights
When people think no one cares
That is when it gets unfair

It hurts me so much to see this sight
It gives me a great big fright
We can change this, so come along
Let's all sing one beautiful song.

Emma Robertson (11)
St Monica's Primary School, Kirkwood

Our Messy World

Clean up all the rubbish.
Put it in a bin.
Then our fight against litter
Will obviously win!

Let us stand up for what is right.
Save the world from our littered streets.
So that we live in a world
That is good and neat!

Whatever the excuse
I don't care,
I don't want to see litter
Anywhere!

Kelsey Cullen (11)
St Monica's Primary School, Kirkwood

Make The War History!

I hear explosions all over the world,
I feel sad, upset and neglected!
I touch the blankets that keep me warm,
I see people die and see dead bodies!
I hope war will end soon!

I hear everything go slow and stop!
I feel happy, excited and relieved,
I touch the ground as I stand on my feet!
I see my friends come to greet me,
I hope the world will stay this way!

Chloe Boyle (11)
St Monica's Primary School, Kirkwood

Being Homeless

If you are homeless,
You live on the street,
You're hungry, you're thin,
With nothing to eat.

It's really sad,
For people out there,
Breathing in the cold,
And really frosty air.

If you don't have a house,
You don't get any heat,
Your toes are cold,
And so are your feet.

I think the council,
Should build more houses,
For homeless people alone,
So they don't have to sleep with the mouses!

Homeless people,
Are very kind.
So the council should give them a house
In good mind.

Sean Fraser (11)
St Monica's Primary School, Kirkwood

Litter, Litter

Litter, litter everywhere
Don't stand there and not care
Pick it up and you will have good luck
Then there will be nothing there
Litter pickers have a hard job
Think twice before you drop
Do it now, pick it up
And never, ever stop!

Shannon Morgan (11)
St Monica's Primary School, Kirkwood

How Long?

How long before everything dies?
How long before trees start to cry?
How long do we have left?
How long until total death?

On the moon, everything is fine,
On the Earth, someone's setting a mine,
Out of all the terrible fights,
Out of all the doves in flight.

When will this mess be fixed?
Will it be later than 2086?
What on earth is going on?
Why on earth has everything gone wrong?

Rachel Mosley (9)
Sandbank Primary School, Dunoon

Eco Code

E njoy the flowers for hours.
C ollect tins for the bins.
O nly one chance.

C are for them, it's up to you.
O zone being destroyed.
D aydream of no litter.
E njoy, don't destroy.

Chloe Carney (9)
Sandbank Primary School, Dunoon

We Have To Save Them Now

Animals are dying
We have to save them now
Tigers, lions, hippos, monkeys
But the question is how?

If you want to save them
We have to stick together
But some habitats and animals
Are endangered by the weather

We have to stop animals dying
At the hands of mankind
If we do, we never know
What changes we will find.

Jack Dempster (11)
Sikeside Primary School, Coatbridge

Litter Poem

Litter is bitter, scattered on the ground,
Every day more litter is found,
Crisp packets and wrappers floating in the air,
Animals are getting hurt everywhere.

Reduce, reuse, recycle,
Don't use the car, walk and cycle,
Use the bins, don't throw stuff around,
Then we'll keep litter off the ground.

Aidan Killen (11)
Sikeside Primary School, Coatbridge

Think About It!

Do not litter, don't be bitter
And take good care of your environment.

Littering is dangerous, littering is mean.
Try to keep your environment clean.

Let's show everyone you are keen,
Do not litter, don't be bitter,
Let's start . . . now!

Linsey Henry (11)
Sikeside Primary School, Coatbridge

Animals Are Going

A nimals
N owhere
I see extinction
M ore animals are dying out
A ll
L ost
S oon will be gone.

A nd will be lost
N o one will see animals.
D o something to help.

E veryone has to help.
'X tinction is bad.
T rees are getting cut down.
I see animals losing their homes.
N ests are falling out of trees.
C utting down the rainforest is bad.
T ime to stop.
I think that we should help.
O ne of the most endangered species is the elephant.
N ever cut down trees.

Alexander Macrae (8)
Strathblane Primary School, Glasgow

Being Homeless

B eing homeless is a doom that falls upon you in the gloom.
E very night, every day, trees get cut down far away.
I n the rainforest, it is green but now there is a huge machine.
N ever mess with these machines because they take away
your dream.
G orillas play in their home for now, and onwards it will fade.

H omeless can be sad for you for there is nothing you can do.
O ur only request is to do our best, and to save the world we try.
M ore and more people cut down trees, that we should try and stop.
E very day and every night
L ess and less people live to see the world all covered in green
and blue.
E very year, every day, there is life all around but some of it
just doesn't stay.
S taring up into space, watching homes fall into waste.
S o after all of this, now you know to help homeless people
in the world.

Alessandro Palmarini & Innis Sherwood-Thompson (8)
Strathblane Primary School, Glasgow

Cars On The Road Of London

I can see cars heading off for work all on the streets of London
I can smell exhaust fumes coming from the cars of London.
I can hear cars turning off and on, all on the streets of London.
I can feel boiling engines coming from cars on the streets of London.
I can help by walking to school every day.

Lucy Taylor Van Nimwegen & Jennifer Cruickshanks (8)
Strathblane Primary School, Glasgow

Reduce, Reuse, Recycle

Reduce
Reuse
Recycle
Save the world
Save the animals
Save the rainforests
Help the homeless
Put the rubbish in the bin
Don't pollute
I like the world
So let's save it.

Calum McCutcheon (8) & Andrew Byles (9)
Strathblane Primary School, Glasgow

You Choose To Reuse

More and more trees are getting killed because we want more paper.
So if we use both sides of the paper we can save some trees.
It's the little things that make a big difference.
If we turn off the lights when we don't need them
we could save lots of power.
If you and loads of your neighbours turn off the tap when you're
brushing your teeth, you could save enough water to fill an Olympic-
sized swimming pool, and if you recycle one aluminium can, you could
save enough electricity to power a TV for three hours.
Did you know that a double-decker bus is the same as forty cars?
So hop on or walk, it's much better for you and the environment
and remember . . . it's the little things that make a big difference!

Alice Ferguson & Grace Currie (9)
Strathblane Primary School, Glasgow

Calling Off Pollution

P overty
O zone layer getting thinner
L itter goes in the bin, not the ground
L et's save the world!'
U se the bins
T ime to stop the world from being polluted
'I 'm hot!'
O ff to stop pollution.
N ow the world is safe!

Conor Haggerty & Martin Riis (8)
Strathblane Primary School, Glasgow

Illness

I llness is caused by
L itter and lost homes and
L ost children. It is becoming a
N ightmare. We need to help the world
E very day or it will go on.
S adly for the world, we must help or we will be
S orry for what we have done.

Fraser Maccorquodale (8)
Strathblane Primary School, Glasgow

Litter

L ots of litter
I t makes me feel sad
T oo much litter
T oo much rubbish
E very day litter drops on the ground
R ubbish wrecks the world so put it in the bin.

Ross McGregor & Eddie Wallace (8)
Strathblane Primary School, Glasgow

Restart Without Pollution

I see vandalism
I see fire in the rainforest
I see animals being used as ornaments
I see hunting nature
I feel global warming
I smell pollution
I see video game violence
I hear people breaking the law
I think some locals pollute this town with gas
I want to start a new life without gases
The environment is dying.

Charlie McCarron & Richard Jack (9)
Strathblane Primary School, Glasgow

Reduce, Reuse, Recycle

R educe, reuse, recycle
E very time you see litter pick it up.
C an you help us?
Y ou can save the world.
C ool!
L ook there's litter
I n the park.
N ow there's no litter.
G ood work!

Erin Orla Howell & Morgan Bernadette Stirton (8)
Strathblane Primary School, Glasgow

Rainforest

People are cutting down trees.
We want to save the rainforest.
Don't cut down trees because they give us oxygen.
Please don't drop litter in the rainforest.

Jessica Collie (9)
Strathblane Primary School, Glasgow

Back Up To Recycle

R ainforest is the home of loads of animals.
E arth must be saved.
C an you save the rainforest?
Y ou can change someone else's life by saving the rainforest.
C ould you please start to recycle?
L isten, you have to recycle!
I hope you've listened.
N ow you know what to do.
G reat is the rainforest!

Adam Wilson (8) & Caspar Schwahn (9)
Strathblane Primary School, Glasgow

Lions

Lions love to lounge around
But soon this pleasure will be gone.
Trees are falling and animals are wailing
At the sound of axes swinging,
Chainsaws chopping
And ploughs ploughing up the forest floor.
Please save this wonderful creature.

Craig Rimmer (10)
Strone of Cally Primary School, Blairgowerie

Racism

R eal people come in
A ll different sizes and
C olours and backgrounds.
I gnorance of cultures means that
S ome people are
M ean to others.

Lewis McLean (8)
The Glasgow Academy Atholl, Glasgow

Behold The Poor Old Polar Bear

Behold the poor old polar bear
Who lives upon the ice
To rob him of this is not fair
Let's be nice and think twice.

Before we use our car
Let's stop and think about it
If we're not going very far
Let's walk and do without it.

Colin MacFarlane (8)
The Glasgow Academy Atholl, Glasgow

Recycling

R ecycling is good for the
E nvironment,
C reate new things.
Y ou can help the environment,
C an you ask other people?
L itter can hurt animals,
I really want to stop it,
N ever drop litter!
G reen is the colour of eco-schools.

Iain Fletcher (7)
The Glasgow Academy Atholl, Glasgow

War

W hy is war so violent?
A re people dying for no good reason?
R est in peace and love.

Jamie Stewart (8)
The Glasgow Academy Atholl, Glasgow

Pollution

P lanes, factories, cars and smoke are bad for the environment.
O n the planet people are dying because of you!
L ook at the mess you've made!
L ook at the rubbish you have dropped!
U nite, we must get together and
T ry and stop it.
I want to stop it
O n planet Earth.
N ow please try and stop it!

Emma Hunter (7)
The Glasgow Academy Atholl, Glasgow

Pollution

Pollution is bad,
Cars, planes and factories make pollution,
Try to stop the fumes.

Try not to make smoking fumes,
If you keep on making pollution it will get worse,
Stop it now!

Mary Potts (8)
The Glasgow Academy Atholl, Glasgow

Recycling

R ecycle, recycle, I do that.
E verybody can recycle.
C an you recycle for the environment?
Y ou can recycle if you try.
C an you clean up the environment?
L itter is bad for the environment.
E ach of us should recycle to save the environment.

Alexander Stewart (8)
The Glasgow Academy Atholl, Glasgow

Litter On The Street

There once was a nice green world,
With nice clean streets,
But what are the streets like today?
The paper that litters on the street
The bubblegum that sticks to your feet,
Who is doing this?
Stop it now!
Stop that paper blowing on the streets.
Stop that bubblegum that sticks to your feet.
Stop it now!
But how?

Mark Wilson (8)
The Glasgow Academy Atholl, Glasgow

The Rainforest

I wish I lived in a rainforest
To see all the plants and animals
I would live with the tribes
And hunt all the food
But I would have to watch out for the snakes in the trees
I would see all the birds in the air
And all the monkeys up in the trees
There would be plants and trees surrounding me.

Jack Henry (8)
The Glasgow Academy Atholl, Glasgow

Litter

People dropping rubbish on the ground,
Animals choking,
Bins overflowing,
Chewing gum all over the pavement,
Cars scattering,
A stench everywhere.

Walter Connolly-Wilkes (7)
The Glasgow Academy Atholl, Glasgow

The Rainforest

Some things are big
Some things are small
But I tell you
The rainforest is tall

The rainforest is disappearing
This is so sad
I wish they would think
Before it gets bad

Do you know
What's going on?
It might be gone
Before too long.

Larissa Lawrie Macaloney (8)
The Glasgow Academy Atholl, Glasgow

The Mountain Gorilla

The mountain gorilla is a peaceful creature
For only eyes to see.
With a big heart and a lovely smile,
The gorilla is just like me.
But why, oh why are you doing this?
Why are they becoming extinct?
So before you kill a gorilla,
Please, please, please stop and think!

Hugo McGregor (8)
The Glasgow Academy Atholl, Glasgow

Racism

Racism means you're judging a person by the colour of their skin.
Why would people be mean to other people
Just because of the colour of their skin?
'Never judge a book by its cover'.

Alice Macintyre-Béon (8)
The Glasgow Academy Atholl, Glasgow

Rainforest

R ainforest has small and tall trees.
A parrot on one of the tall trees.
I wonder if I can be a monkey,
N ot a chimpanzee.
F or all the lovely trees I wish I could see.
O f the work of the tree-killer, the
R ainforest, you and me will never see.
E ven the monkeys will find nothing to
S wing on.
T he lovely rainforest is in danger.

Georgia Dunn (9)
The Glasgow Academy Atholl, Glasgow

Litter

Lots of litter on the ground,
It is really damaging our town.
It's hurting the animals,
Can't you see?
Even though we're trying to keep it clean.
So stop all this
And think aloud,
Don't drop litter
On the ground.

Alexandra Ava Barber (8)
The Glasgow Academy Atholl, Glasgow

War

W hy is this happening?
A ll our villages are exploding.
R un, run, run for your life.

Trevor Ace (7)
The Glasgow Academy Atholl, Glasgow

My Pet Snake

I love my pet snake
When he's lying on the ground
Eating all the mice
That his best friend found.

Once he was slithering
Through the trees
Then he saw a monkey
And bit it on the knees.

Some snakes are big
Some snakes are small
Once I had a snake
Climb up my wall.

Jack James McCready (8)
The Glasgow Academy Atholl, Glasgow

Litter On Our Streets

Some people think
They can throw litter away
Without hurting animals
But they *do!* So stop it now
Stop it now
For everyone's sake
Give us a break!
You're hurting animals
For goodness sake
Think of the foxes
Think of the cubs
So just put your rubbish in the bin
And keep our streets nice and clean.

Robyn Spalding (8)
The Glasgow Academy Atholl, Glasgow

Rainforests

R ainforests, rainforests
A re our friends
I n this world
N othing good is happening
F or all the animals will be destroyed
O h! Why are you destroying
R ainforests? They provide us with food to
E at. I am telling you to
S top it now. Don't kill those
T igers - don't kill anything.
S ave the rainforests please!

Gordon Stackhouse (8)
The Glasgow Academy Atholl, Glasgow

Litter

Litter, litter on the ground,
Litter, litter all around,
Who is dumping all this muck,
All over our streets? *Oh yuck!*

People, people laughing at clowns,
People, people cleaning up towns.
Volunteer to clean up streets,
To volunteer is no fear.

Litter, litter on the ground,
Litter, litter all around.
Why are we being bad?
Can't you see it's making us sad?

Litter, litter off the ground,
Litter, litter not around.
The town is clear,
You don't have to volunteer. *Hooray!*

Ruairidh Russell (8)
The Glasgow Academy Atholl, Glasgow

Rainforest

Rainforests, rainforests everywhere,
Monkeys swinging in the air,
Snakes slithering down and down,
Trying to catch the bugs.

Toucans flying way up high,
Jaguars crawling slowly by.
Butterflies flying in the air,
So beautiful I stop and stare.

Parrots going down to land,
Trying to catch a juicy spider.
The spider tries to get away,
See you another day!

Sophie Pell (8)
The Glasgow Academy Atholl, Glasgow

Rainforest

R ainforests are good for
A reason if you could believe
I n rainforests you get medicine
N ow bad people are destroying rain
F orests, so please help stop the
O help the environment
R ecycle cans and plastic bottles
E nvironmentally friendly
S o
T his is what to do!

Rajeshwar Dhami (8)
The Glasgow Academy Atholl, Glasgow

Litter

Litter, litter everywhere,
Some people don't even care.
Whatever you do,
Be aware,
Because some people love this planet,
So please don't drop your packets.
Litter, litter everywhere,
On the street and on the stairs.
One day you'll stop and stare,
What you are doing is wrong!

Katie Watson (8)
The Glasgow Academy Atholl, Glasgow

War - Haikus

W ars are dangerous,
A ll guns and bombs must be stopped,
R emember that now.

W ars must be stopped now,
A ll of the guns can kill you,
R emember that now.

W hy do they do it?
A re they trying to kill us?
R emember that now.

Judith Arbuckle (7)
The Glasgow Academy Atholl, Glasgow

The Rainforests Are Dying

The rainforests were growing up and up,
But now they are coming down and down.
There is no point for this,
It is such a waste of time.

Birds, butterflies and lots more are dying.
Stop this!
It is a dreadful habit.
Why is this happening?

Stop, I say
Stop, and I mean stop!
The planet is shrinking bit by bit.
That is why I say stop!
The rainforests are nearly gone
So *stop!*

Ruth Miller (9)
The Glasgow Academy Atholl, Glasgow

Rainforest

Some trees are big
Some trees are small
Some of them might fall
And the rainforest is tall
Don't cut the trees
Don't waste paper at all
Keep the rainforest healthy
Please don't cut the trees down
Don't hurt the animals.

Morna Ruth Sinclair (8)
The Glasgow Academy Atholl, Glasgow

In The Rainforest

R ound the corner I saw
A snake which was green and red
I t was slithering through
N oisy, crunchy leaves, a huge
F orest tree coming
O ver me, then I saw a
R hinoceros
E ating grass
S nakes were slithering up my leg
T hey were slimy.

Luca Giovanazzi (8)
The Glasgow Academy Atholl, Glasgow

Pollution

P lanet Earth is dying
O ur animals will die
L et us help
L ove planet Earth
U s who are going to be killed
T he future depends on us
I t will have pollution
O h help!
N ow help!

Zander Grant (7)
The Glasgow Academy Atholl, Glasgow

Young Writers Information

We hope you have enjoyed reading this book - and that you will continue to enjoy it in the coming years.

If you like reading and writing poetry drop us a line, or give us a call, and we'll send you a free information pack.

Alternatively if you would like to order further copies of this book or any of our other titles, then please give us a call or log onto our website at www.youngwriters.co.uk

**Young Writers Information
Remus House
Coltsfoot Drive
Peterborough
PE2 9JX**

(01733) 890066